A LEADERSHIP GUIDE FOR WOMEN
IN HIGHER EDUCATION

T0373149

A Leadership Guide *for* Women *in* Higher Education

MARJORIE HASS

JOHNS HOPKINS UNIVERSITY PRESS | *Baltimore*

© 2021 Johns Hopkins University Press
All rights reserved. Published 2021
Printed in the United States of America on acid-free paper
2 4 6 8 9 7 5 3

Johns Hopkins University Press
2715 North Charles Street
Baltimore, Maryland 21218-4363
www.press.jhu.edu

Library of Congress Cataloging-in-Publication Data

Names: Hass, Marjorie, 1965– author.
Title: A leadership guide for women in higher education / Marjorie Hass.
Description: Baltimore : Johns Hopkins University Press, 2021. | Includes
bibliographical references and index.
Identifiers: LCCN 2020033842 | ISBN 9781421441016 (paperback) | ISBN
9781421441023 (ebook)
Subjects: LCSH: Women in higher education—Vocational guidance—Handbooks,
manuals, etc.
Classification: LCC LC1557 .H37 2021 | DDC 378.0082—dc23
LC record available at https://lccn.loc.gov/2020033842

A catalog record for this book is available from the British Library.

*Special discounts are available for bulk purchases of this book. For more information,
please contact Special Sales at specialsales@jh.edu.*

For Peyton "Randy" Helm

CONTENTS

Acknowledgments   ix

Introduction   1

1. Transforming Your Professional
Identity   14

2. Navigating Power and Conflict   34

3. Finding Joy in Your Work   53

4. Growing as a Leader   66

5. Crafting a Vision   89

6. Building Your Skills   105

7. Winning the Job   117

Concluding Thoughts   144

Notes   147
Index   149

ACKNOWLEDGMENTS

This book is deeply grounded in my experiences as a leader. As a result, I owe a debt to all those who have supported me and my work over the past two decades.

Many extraordinary leaders believed in me and offered me opportunities to lead. And then they stood by me with support, wise counsel, and friendship. I would like to thank in particular Cary Fowler, Randy Helm, Robert Johnson, Bill Michaelcheck, Jim Steffy, and Todd Williams. Each of these men models courageous leadership and has been a strong advocate for creating opportunities for women and others.

I have been fortunate to work closely with talented senior leadership teams at Muhlenberg College, Austin College, and Rhodes College. Our work together has brought me great satisfaction and created life-long bonds. I have learned from every one of these colleagues and count each of them as a friend and advisor.

Among the many satisfactions of academic leadership is the chance to collaborate with other people across institutions. During my service on the boards of the Council of Independent Colleges, the National Association of Independent Colleges and Universities, and the Association of American Colleges and Universities, I was fortunate to work side by side with presidents and other academic leaders from all over the country from whom I learned, and continue to learn, a great deal. I thank Rich Ekman, Lynn Pasquerella, and David Warren for their transformative national leadership and for the invitation to join them in this important work.

The provosts and presidents of the Annapolis Group create a collegial community. Much of what I know about being an effective president has been gained from Annapolis conversations. The formal presentations are important, but so too are the warm companionship, the laughter, the frank disclosures over a glass of wine, and the deep friendships that are formed.

I am grateful to the women who participated in my seminars and who invited me into their lives as leaders. They have been a source of support, learning, and development. It is a joy to know them and to watch them develop as leaders. The questions and values they brought to our shared work shaped every stage of this book.

Several colleagues read versions of chapters along the way, and their advice has made this a better book. I would particularly like to thank a group of very wise women: Meredith Davis, Amy Jasperson, Sue May, Michelle Meyer, Lisa Perfetti, Randi Tanglen, and Angela Webster.

I am grateful to Johns Hopkins University Press for publishing this book. Greg Britton encouraged me to write it and has been a supportive and thoughtful editor. Barbara Kline Pope offered early enthusiastic support as well. Anonymous readers offered helpful suggestions on behalf of the press.

The faculty summer writing group at Rhodes College gave me energy to write the first draft of the manuscript. Those weekly gentle check-ins with colleagues helped me to prioritize writing.

I am fortunate to have a supportive family cheering section. The Hoit, Hass, Lee, Stuller, and Schick clans are a source of ongoing inspiration, love, and support. My husband, Larry, is a friend to my passions and the love of my life. He never doubted that this book mattered, and he never flagged in his encouragement as I wrote it. Our children—Cameron, Katie, and Jessica—support me in my work even as they remind me that work is only one part of my life. I am so grateful to them and for them.

A LEADERSHIP GUIDE FOR WOMEN
IN HIGHER EDUCATION

Introduction

———

FOR MANY YEARS I was approached by women in higher education for advice and support as they took on leadership roles and navigated their career paths. By 2013 the number of women wanting this kind of mentoring had outpaced my ability to provide it one-on-one. I began offering online seminars so I could meet with women in small groups to answer questions and encourage them to develop mutually supportive relationships. In these seminars, I worked with women at almost every career stage and with a wide range of titles and responsibilities. Some were already vice presidents about to make the decision to pursue a presidency. Others were mid-career, ready for their first big supervisory role. Still others were at an early career stage, intrigued by the possibility of a future in academic leadership and wondering how to prepare. The participants came from every corner of higher education: academic affairs, student affairs, admissions, athletics, development, accrediting agencies, and on and on. And they brought experience in different types of institutions from large research universities to regional public universities to liberal arts colleges to community colleges. In our conversations we found that even though we differed in our career paths and sectors, we were united by common questions about how leadership works in higher education and how women lead.

From the beginning, the workshops had a unique tone driven by the concerns of the participants. Most of the current books and seminars aimed at prospective academic leaders focus on skill development. But the women who approached me for advice were not just looking for help learning how to forecast a budget or ask for a major gift. Their questions were deeper and more personal. They wanted to know what it feels like to lead, what it requires emotionally and spiritually, and what kinds of personal sacrifices are necessary. For these women, there is no neat distinction between "work" and "life." As they contemplated whether to take up the mantle of academic leadership, they wanted to understand what it means from the inside.

This book is a distillation of the discussions I have led in my online workshops and of the hundreds of informal conversations I have had with women throughout higher education. Some of the issues I discuss in this book are specifically women's concerns—focused on what it means to lead from the downside of the patriarchal hierarchy. Other issues are ones that every leader should think through but that women seem more likely to articulate and address. Although I center the issues that most directly emerge from women's concerns, my hope is that there is something useful here for men as well.

I write from my lived experience as a straight, cis, white woman who is aware that women who don't inhabit these categories face pressures, challenges, and joys that I cannot directly know. I have been fortunate to have a diverse group of women in my seminars, and I have learned a great deal from each of them. I have also asked several friends to read drafts of this book and to offer interventions and insights drawn from their own diverse experiences. I am grateful for this advice and support and hopeful that they have helped me make this book useful to a wider range of women.

I have spent my career at small liberal arts colleges, and that naturally affects my perspective. I have used what I have learned from the women in my workshops who have built careers in larger and/or public institutions. But there are likely spots in this book where readers from other branches of higher ed will need to test my assumptions against what they know to be true in their own context.

My Path to the Presidency

Like many college presidents, I didn't start with serving as president as a career goal. I was attached to my discipline (philosophy), my students, and my research agenda. After gaining admission to graduate school, my first professional goal was to complete a dissertation and earn a PhD. After that, I wanted to get a tenure-track job, earn tenure, and then advance to the rank of full professor. My ambitions were faculty-based, and I ultimately achieved each of these goals as I rose through the ranks at Muhlenberg College. But by the time I was promoted to full professor, I was also serving as provost. I hadn't seen this coming, but in retrospect it makes sense that my career pivoted in this way.

From the beginning, I had taken leadership roles on faculty committees, often because "we need a woman." Even as a junior faculty member, I served on the budget advisory committee, sitting with senior vice presidents as they developed the college's macro budget and learning early on how the business side of the college functioned. In committee work and, later, directing Muhlenberg's Center for Ethics, I discovered how much I liked being part of a team and working with others to achieve goals. I also found that I had a knack for getting things done in ways that didn't alienate others. And I liked being able to see the big picture and make an institutional impact.

Surprisingly, some of the parts of myself that weren't important in my work as an academic turned out to be keys to success in public leadership roles. For example, my generally cheerful disposition, my sense of humor and quick way with words, my personal style, my identity as a wife and mother—in the context of administrative work all of these were more than just the neutral attributes they had been in my career as a professor. As a leader representing the college publicly and working across departments and divisions, they were valuable traits that helped me to work effectively.

A turning point in my career came when Randy Helm, just arrived as president of Muhlenberg College, invited me to apply for the newly created role of provost. At that time, I was serving as interim dean of the college, a position I had anticipated lasting only a year. As I thought about whether to leap into the competitive search process, I realized that this decision was about much more than my career narrowly understood. This was a decision that had implications for how I saw myself—my core identity—and for the way my husband and I saw our family's future. I needed to gauge my fortitude for entering into a search process where I would be an internal candidate with no guarantee of success. Could I handle the disappointment and embarrassment of being turned down? Was I only being invited into the pool so they could say they considered a woman? Would I lose some of my faculty friends?

I needed to think through the impact this would have on my family if I was successful. This was more than just a matter of the time the new role would take. It was about our future. I was only thirty-seven years old. If I became provost, it was impossible to imagine I would hold that position until retirement. Likely I would need to physically move for my next job—and move my family along with me. Were we prepared for that? How would it affect my husband's work? He was also a tenured faculty member at the same institution. Would he mind that I was stepping away from our shared work as professors? What might it do to our equitable relationship that I would be taking a leap forward in my earning potential? Finally, I knew it would be hard to go back to being a faculty member after serving as provost. Was I prepared to take on a new professional identity? Was I prepared to relinquish the old one?

A long talk with my husband helped me decide to throw my hat in the ring. He offered his full support and assured me that he would adapt to my new role and would comfort and love me if I wasn't successful. His confidence in me was contagious and helped me find the courage to take the risk.

That first big decision and the questions it raised for me continue to inform my work as I assist other women in their own career journeys. As I got to know my male counterparts, I learned that their discernment process about career advancement was very different than mine. They weren't racked about shifting identities. They weren't conflicted about their ambition or worried that they might lose a friend. They were confident about their talents and usually felt they deserved the job. And while most (but not all) were sensitive to the impact of a potential move on their families, they seemingly gave no thought at all to the ways money, power, and identity could change their relationships.

Leading as a Woman

Taking on the role of provost at Muhlenberg made me the first woman—and the first Jewish person—to serve as the college's chief academic officer. This status as the first of my kind followed me to my presidencies at Austin College and Rhodes College. From the beginning, these facts were regularly included in introductions and in articles about my work. I initially resisted this emphasis on my personal identity as a Jewish woman and found myself irritated by how often this was mentioned or remarked upon. I worried that the constant attention to my gender and my religion would detract from more pertinent aspects of my work. I worried as well that it made my institutions look out of date—the celebration of a white woman's rise to the top only highlighted how long it had taken and how women and men of color had not yet been allowed to ascend.

But it didn't take long for me to realize that breaking through these glass ceilings was about far more than my individual achievement. By inhabiting these leadership positions, I inevitably served as a positive role model for others and as a symbol of what was possible. I began to make expanding opportunities for others an explicit part of my leadership agenda. By speaking about my own walk through a new door, I could hold the doors open even wider for those who come after me. At a time when women outpace men in college enrollment and achievement and when the population of college-age students is becoming increasingly diverse, I feel a responsibility to do all I can to diversify academic leadership. Embracing my identity as the "first woman"—and a Jewish woman as well—at my institutions is a step toward that goal.

For me and for the women who talk with me about their academic leadership careers, moving up the ladder is a personal as well as a professional climb. It is also an act of resistance in the face of explicit and implicit sexism and, for many, racism or heterosexism. Barriers to women's achievement are ubiquitous. In addition to egregious examples of abusive behavior (highlighted by the social media hashtag #MeToo), I regularly hear of women who are doing the hard work while a man holds the formal title, of women passed over as too old while their male counterpart is lauded as experienced, and of women's promotions hinging on accomplishment while a man gets promoted based on his potential. Women still have to contend with the dissonance between normative femininity and the expectations of leadership. We are still more likely to take on the "second shift" of caring for the home and to be the ones navigating the needs of children and older parents. And we are still expected to smile more and be nicer than men in similar roles.

Leading in spite of these obstacles is possible. From those leadership positions, we can do more than leap over or work around barriers. We can lead in ways that dismantle them, making a fairer playing field for those who come after us. Sometimes, the experiences and strengths we have as women make us better leaders. Sometimes, our experiences just wear us out. Either way, women's leadership makes a tremendous, positive difference. According to a CNBC report, companies with women at the highest leadership levels produce more net profit and produce more patents.[1] *Forbes* reported on research by the Korn Ferry Institute that showed that women CEOs score higher than their male counterparts on several leadership traits, including risk taking, agility, resilience, and coping with ambiguity.[2] Whether these differences are the results of socialization, innate tendencies, or having more diverse perspectives at the decision-making table, they are a reminder that higher education as a whole benefits when women take leadership roles.

My goal in this book is to help other women advance in their careers and to expand the range of voices leading the way in higher education. I hope to assist and affirm women who are considering moving into leadership roles. And I hope to help those who are already there as they consider the next step toward a deanship, a vice presidency, or a presidency.

The women in my seminars often wonder if they are "ready" to advance. They aren't sure how to assess their own qualifications. They aren't always sure how to own their ambition. This was my experience too. Years ago, while serving as a provost, I was surprised to find out that many of my male peers were attending workshops about preparing for the presidency. Ads and invitations for pre-presidential programs came across my desk fairly regularly, but it had never occurred to me to apply for any of them. At the time, it would have struck me as presumptuous. Who was I to think I could be a college president? Didn't I need to wait for someone to anoint me rather than just raise my hand? And how would I tell others that I was hoping to advance in this way? Apparently, my male colleagues had no such qualms.

I recognize now that my reluctance to consider pre-presidential workshops was part of an overall ambivalence about my ambition. I had successfully earned a PhD, tenure, and promotion to full professor. On the surface, it might have seemed that I was comfortable with my own desire to succeed. But I had managed to reach those goals without having to give them much thought and without having to step beyond what others around me were doing. I was fortunate to come from an educated family, and so the decision to go to graduate school didn't feel particularly ambitious. Once there, I did what was expected in order to get to the next stage in a career that has pretty well-defined steps. I was hardworking and goal-oriented, but I didn't think of myself as having big ambitions or taking risks in my career.

I was fortunate to meet several people who encouraged me at that point in my career: Jim Steffy, then interim president of Muhlenberg

College; Randy Helm, now president emeritus of Muhlenberg College; Shelly Storbeck of Storbeck/Pimentel; and Tom Courtice, then president of Academic Search. Each of them offered support and enthusiasm about what I could bring to a presidency. Without this explicit support, I am not sure I would have moved forward—at least not as quickly and successfully as I did.

In this book I am paying this support forward by offering other women encouragement and an inside look at what is required for effective leadership. I hope that women will read and discuss this book together. There is no substitute for the powerful community women can make when we gather in the spirit of self-discovery and mutual support. The beautiful concept of "lift as we rise" (drawn from the African American experience) is one of my personal mottos. It reminds me that there is no individual success, no individual accomplishment that means more than ensuring that we leave the doors open wider for those who follow in our wake.

As I wrote this book, I imagined that I was in conversation with the many women who have approached me for advice and mentoring over the years. As in those face-to-face encounters, I am drawing on my experience to provide advice, support, and ideas for deepening reflection. This is a personal book. My advice is not meant to be canonical, and it isn't based on formal research. I offer my current and best thinking and invite you to consider it and take only what is useful to you. Academic leadership is endlessly challenging. I do not consider my own learning complete. Often, the advice I offer to others turns out to be the exact piece of counsel I myself need. And even more often, I learn and grow from the wisdom of the women who seek my advice.

In these pages, I emphasize the concept of leadership. In fact, I rarely use the word "administrator" to describe the work I do or the work that women are hoping to do as they take on roles such as associate dean, athletic director, dean, provost, vice president, or president. An administrator carries out functions: she creates a schedule, applies a rule, or fills out a form. Every senior role includes administrative functions, which are often tedious but are necessary. But the real work—the work that requires judgment, vision, and creativity—

is much more than paper pushing or carrying out premade decisions. The real work is the work of leading.

It is a rare day when those in senior positions are described by those on campus as "leaders," but that is the heart of what we do. Chapter 4 is devoted to an analysis of leadership in the academic context. For now, I simply encourage you to think of yourself as a current or future leader and to use this term often and with pride.

At the same time, we have to recapture "administrator" as a positive role. Faculty, staff, and students talk—often in a disparaging tone—about "the administration." It is a catchall term for the people who have the power to make decisions, and it is most often used when the speaker is unhappy with the decision that has been made. As a mass term, it allows the speaker to be critical without naming a specific person. The way the term is often used conjures up a Kafkaesque image of meaningless control. The "administration" is a nameless, faceless wall of "no." Administrators are (empty) suits. They don't understand the real needs of the college. Their decisions are not grounded in wise reflection but rather in the desire to exercise power over others.

We can resist this stereotype by asking people to individuate. When someone says "the administration" to me, I ask them to tell me about whom they are speaking. It is usually a single dean or an individual staff member. Sometimes, they mean me. Once they stop using "the administration" as a euphemism, we are in the realm of the human instead of the abstract. It is harder to make a stereotype stick to an actual person. It is then easier to get to the root of the concern.

Another way to resist the stereotype is to speak more often about the process by which we make decisions. Shining a light on the complexity of our administrative work helps to demystify it so that others can understand our practices and principles. Taking the time to express care for individuals and to reiterate the values of the institution brings the work of the administration into the fabric of the mission of the college rather than positioning it in opposition.

Leadership is a personal and spiritual journey. Being a vice president or president makes it impossible to ignore your own strengths and weaknesses. You see both reflected back to you every day. Learning to welcome this knowledge and to seek ever-greater self-discovery has made me a better leader.

A Word about Mentoring

I am often approached by women who are anxious because they do not have a mentor or who are hoping that I will mentor them or help them find a mentor. I sense their underlying belief that a mentor is necessary if they are to succeed. This isn't so. Many leaders—including me—didn't have a specific person who served as a mentor.

A true mentoring relationship is intense and highly focused. Asking someone to be your mentor is a big request: you are asking them to devote time and energy to you and your career. It isn't something that can be lightly undertaken. Most genuine mentoring relationships develop naturally over time and because there is sympathy, affection, and respect between the two parties. If you are fortunate to have a mentor, express your gratitude regularly. But do not despair if this kind of relationship is not available to you. There are other valuable relationships that are easier to develop and that will help you advance.

One such relationship is with an advisor or supporter. I have had many of these people in my life, and this is how I think of my relationships with the women in my seminars. They know I am available for advice and support, and they can call on me when they need to even though we do not have a deeper, ongoing mentoring relationship. They understand that my time is limited, and they do not take advantage of my willingness to respond to a call or an email. I deeply value these relationships and do my best to assist when called upon. Asking someone for a specific piece of advice is almost always appropriate—and sometimes even flattering. You should feel free to reach out occasionally to others without worrying that you are imposing or asking for too much of their time or energy.

Another important kind of relationship to cultivate is a sponsoring one. A sponsor will recommend you, connect you to others, and make sure you are in the room where things are happening. Here, too, I have been fortunate. A sponsor calls you when opportunities arise and thinks of you when she is asked for recommendations or nominations. Since the sponsor is putting her own reputation on the line, this is a slightly deeper relationship than with an advisor or supporter, but it is also relatively easy to develop. I have served as this kind of sponsor for many of the women in my seminars and many others I have met in a variety of situations. If you have proven your talents to someone, it is usually fine to let them know that you are interested in a certain set of experiences or positions and ask them to keep you in mind should they hear of opportunities.

Remember as well that wherever you are in your career, you have the opportunity—indeed, the responsibility—to serve as a mentor, advisor, and sponsor. Doing so will help others and will help you grow as a leader.

Outline of the Book

I anticipate that readers are at various points in their careers and coming from a variety of areas within higher education. I have tried to write in a way that will be useful to you all. Often, faculty members have the biggest jump to make when they move into senior administration because the work is so different from teaching and scholarship. Coaches have a similar hurdle to jump to become an athletic director. Other readers will be used to doing administrative work and to being accountable to and for others. I acknowledge these differences in the chapters where it is relevant. I have organized this book to be read either cover to cover or as a resource for specific questions.

The early chapters focus on the internal process of taking on a leadership role and the impact on self and identity. Chapter 1, "Transforming Your Professional Identity," addresses the issues that most often bring women into my seminars. Those who have recently taken on a new leadership role wrestle with the surprising dislocation that occurs as their sense of professional identity undergoes a massive shift. Those anticipating such a career move are often wary of what it will mean for their personal relationships. Issues of identity and transition are foundational for successfully navigating leadership, and they are where my seminars usually begin.

Chapter 2, "Navigating Power and Conflict," addresses areas that are often challenging for women. Having been socialized to disown our power and to avoid conflict, we may be unprepared for the strong feelings that emerge in ourselves and in others in response to our new, more powerful professional role. In my seminars, these topics generate a lot of "aha" moments as we share stories of our emerging abilities to take on conflict and difficult emotions.

Chapter 3, "Finding Joy in Your Work," is in part an answer to the question, Why would anyone want to lead, given how hard it is? Finding joy in the midst of what is often stressful work is an art—one that has to be cultivated. I offer a variety of ways to focus on and expand your capacity to experience your work as a source of deep pleasure.

The second portion of the book turns to an analysis of the work itself. I offer my insights into the nature of academic leadership and share hard-earned advice about how to do it successfully. Chapter 4, "Growing as a Leader," responds to the many questions I receive about how to lead effectively and with integrity. Women often lack role models for how to lead *as a woman,* that is, without adopting the worst of masculine power dynamics. Focusing on how to inspire positive change is one way I encourage women to carve their own path.

Chapter 5, "Crafting a Vision," offers inspirational and practical advice for one of the most important but least understood leadership skills. Visioning is often highly creative and hence is a fulfilling part of leadership, but there are few resources devoted to understanding or honing this skill. Women have the opportunity to bring their own experiences of exclusion to this work and to build visions that are widely inclusive and influential.

Finally, I focus on the practicalities of a woman moving forward in her career, advice I am often asked to provide. In chapter 6, "Building Your Skills," I identify the key initial and advanced skills required for that next position. Chapter 7, "Winning the Job," gives a detailed overview of the search process as well as advice about how to decide whether to enter a search. These chapters provide a guide to assessing your current skill level and planning your next move.

A Leadership Moment

I am completing this book in the midst of several interrelated critical events: the COVID-19 pandemic, an economic recession, and an uprising in the name of Black Lives Matter. Higher education is implicated in each of these as a part of the problem and as an essential part of the solution. If we are to build a more equitable world—one in which economic, educational, and political power is not systematically hoarded—our colleges and universities have to participate in radical, structural change. This work will be painful, joyful, frightening, uplifting, and disruptive. We must embrace it in all of its contradictions and complexities.

I hope this book inspires women and others to step forward and take on the responsibilities of leading. I hope it inspires all of us to follow the leadership of Black women and others whose lived experience, research, and brilliance can show us ways to remake ourselves and our institutions. The future of higher education depends on it.

1

Transforming Your
Professional Identity

———

IF YOU ARE READING this book, it is likely that you are considering moving into a leadership role or advancing from the one you have now. Perhaps a job ad has caught your attention. Or your supervisor has complimented you on the initiatives you brought to the department and suggested you are ready for a promotion. Or a senior leader on your campus has said they would like to nominate you for a deanship. Whatever the impetus, you find yourself imagining what it would be like to move into a senior leadership position.

You might be stirred to act for a variety of reasons. The women in my seminars are typically excited about the opportunity to make a broad and positive difference for students. They believe that higher education is a path to social justice. They want to transform an institution so that it can better serve its mission. They have discovered that leadership is a form of service, that it matters who leads, and that they could have a meaningful impact.

These internal desires to inspire others and to make change are the best kinds of motivation. More mundane, material concerns shouldn't be discounted, but they can't be your only motivation. The perceived perks—a nicer office, a higher salary, a fancier title—aren't enough to compensate for the hard work it takes to lead. Similarly, while external promptings are flattering, meeting the hopes or expectations others have for you won't be sustaining in the long run. Without a mission and service orientation, leadership positions are empty and unfulfilling. The happiest leaders see themselves as subordinate to a higher purpose.

But even the call to lead isn't enough on its own. Women know that senior leadership positions come with a host of challenges. These jobs are time-consuming, often thankless, and usually stressful. Pursuing a big leadership role means changes in how you live, whom you spend time with, and how you think about your career. The academic version of the c-suite may beckon to you, but before you head toward it, you likely want a better understanding of what it will mean.

I hear again and again from women as they wrestle with this decision. They are aware that a deanship or a vice presidency will change their lives, but they aren't sure how. They want to understand what these roles feel like from the inside. Will the work be fulfilling? Will it be lonely? Who will I be once I hold this new title?

This chapter is about what happens to your identity when you take a senior leadership position. If you are like me and the women with whom I have worked, you may find that this change in job status marks an equally significant change in your sense of self and your professional identity. If you are thinking about whether you want to be a senior administrator, reflecting on what it will mean for you personally can help you make a better decision. If you have recently been promoted, this kind of reflection can help you get your bearings and make sense of the shifts that have occurred in your life.

In my seminars, I describe the move into a full-time, upper-level administrative role as "the jump." This short phrase is a reminder that what we are talking about is a difference in kind and not just degree. It isn't a matter of just inching ahead on a known path; it is a pretty radical change of paths. What lies on the other side of the jump is much more than a new title or a new set of responsibilities. It is a new way of understanding yourself and your relationship to your work.

The jump gets made in different ways depending on your institution and your particular career path. In academic affairs and student affairs, the first jump is likely to be an appointment as a dean or vice president. For women in physical education, it could be an appointment as an athletic director or associate athletic director. Titles vary in other areas, but what they have in common is that you are leaving behind frontline work where you were teaching, coaching, or directly serving students—where you were a practitioner—and moving into a job where your primary responsibility is to lead a division, unit, or school.

You may have eased into the jump, serving as a department chair or as the senior women's athletic administrator while still teaching or coaching. You may have moved up through student affairs by taking on more and more managerial responsibilities. Or you may be jumping right into the deep end as a dean or provost. But whether you have been moving up gradually or are making a sudden career swerve, the transition changes your life.

The jump seems to be most disorienting for those of us who come out of the faculty. If you are a faculty member, your primary professional identity is likely tied to your discipline. You may have chosen this field in college and since then been on a fairly rigid track. When you were promoted from assistant to associate professor, you were probably relieved and maybe excited about the job security and the public affirmation. But it didn't make a significant difference to your day-to-day work or sense of professional identity. You were still a faculty member, and other than a modest raise, the opportunity for some new committee assignments, and sabbatical eligibility, not much really changed. So too with promotion to full professor. Your first full-time administrative assignment, on the other hand, changes just about every aspect of your work and your life. It requires you to engage in radically different tasks than those that made up your professorial portfolio of teaching, research, and college service.

After the jump, everything is different: how much control you have over your time, whom you think of as your peer group, what you wear, how your income affects your family, and what it means to succeed.

The holistic nature of this shift is disorienting and is the source of much of the anxiety and questions that women bring to me.

The jump inaugurates *changes* in your circumstances and a *transition* in your identity. This distinction is described by William Bridges in his thoughtful book, *The Way of Transition*. He points out that change is situational—you get a new job or move to a new institution. Transition, on the other hand, is the internal process that allows you to remake yourself in response to change.[1]

Bridges argues that a successful transition doesn't happen all at once. It unfolds over time and requires a first period of letting go, a second liminal period, and then a final period when the new identity emerges and solidifies. You will likely go through this three-part transition process as part of your first big jump and then possibly again and again as your career moves forward.

As Bridges notes, shifts in identity take time to be internalized. Change and transition don't happen at the same time. Usually change comes first: you take a new job or you move across the country. The transition comes a bit later as you adapt to your new role or location and start to feel like you belong. Transitions can be smooth or bumpy, easy or hard. But they can't be avoided.

It can be disorienting to take a new job and suddenly find yourself regretting what you left behind. This is a normal part of any successful transition. In the midst of shedding an old identity, it is common to feel regret and loss. For women, it also seems to be a time to experience impostor syndrome, becoming beset with worry that someone will find out they aren't really meant for this work. When I get a call from a woman in this stage of transition, she is often wondering, What have I done? Why did I give up my old job? I advise her that acknowledging the losses diminishes their potency. It then becomes easier to remember the reasons for her decision and the positive ways her life has changed.

When I first became a provost, I had a recurring dream that I had been invited to a dinner party and then discovered that no place had been set for me. These dreams made me aware of how lonely I felt now that I was no longer part of a faculty. Over the years, I have found that dreams like this are common during the transitional period.

Even when you are definitely ready for a change and your period of mourning is brief, the middle stage of transition can leave you feeling dislocated. You aren't sure if you fit into this new life even though you no longer can hold on to the old one. If you are in the midst of the somewhat dark night of liminality, I encourage you to recognize that even though it can be difficult, it is also precious and important. Embrace the dislocation rather than hiding from it. Soon enough, you will no longer be a stranger in your new job; for now, appreciate the insights that "beginner's mind" can offer. Since you are not yet an insider, you will see things that are invisible to those around you. Write down everything you find unusual—both the good and the bad. These notes will serve you well in later months when you have more fully adapted to the culture, and its particularities are less visible. Often your most important initiatives will have their seeds in the dislocation you experienced as you stood between the worlds of your old job and your new one.

In my own career, reflected in the conversations I have with other women, I have come to see the jump not simply as a single giant transition, but as a series of smaller ones. Not every woman experiences the same ones. If you come from the professoriate, the jump might feel wider than if you are being promoted from within the ranks of student life professionals. The magnitude of the jump depends as well on the nature of your new position. The presidency, for example, is more public than other roles.

The following list of potential transitions is an overview. These seem to require the most thought and raise the most questions for women. The first five are particularly aimed at faculty members and other people moving into an administrative position for the first time. The middle five are more generally applicable. The final four refer specifically to the presidency. Please take this opportunity to reflect on the transitions that are most salient to you.

transition from autonomy to teamwork
transition from a shared path to individual ambition
transition from expert to generalist

transition from colleague to employee
transition from colleague to boss
transition from individual to symbol
transition from earner to breadwinner
transition from dressing for yourself to executive style
transition from "front of the house" to "back of the house"
transition from group identity to a tighter network
transition from having a boss to reporting to a board
transition from one among many to sui generis
transition from private citizen to public figure
transition from a job to a lifestyle

Some of these topics are covered in detail in later chapters, but for now, here is a brief description of each one. I include some questions for reflection and discussion as a way of helping you decide if you are ready to make the jump. If you have already jumped, the questions may help you think more deeply about what you have gone through and what might lie ahead.

Faculty to Administration Transitions

Many—possibly most—academic leaders begin their careers as faculty members. They bring with them a deep, internalized understanding of the work faculty do and the way this work shapes one's professional identity. The transition from faculty member to administrator may be common, but it can be difficult since administrative work requires giving up many of the things that make faculty work compelling. Adjusting to these losses and adapting to a new, exciting role takes energy and time.

From Autonomy to Teamwork

The transition from autonomy to teamwork is particularly acute for women who come from the faculty or from other areas where autonomy is the norm, such as athletics or counseling. As a faculty member, you choose what projects to work on, what to teach, and when you will do your work. Within a relatively thin framework, you have a lot of control about how you use your time. You are part of a department, but that department isn't primarily a team: you don't set major shared goals or keep each other regularly apprised of your work. You have a department chair, but she isn't monitoring you or making unilateral decisions about how you spend your day. Most of the big decisions about how to do your job happen independently of your chair and your department.

But after the jump, you are a member of a team and are expected to support the group's direction and decisions. You set shared goals and work on projects together. Your work has to fit in with the work of others, and there are few decisions you can make without consulting with people in your office or on your team.

As a faculty member, you can grumble all you want about your department chair or a departmental decision you disagree with. But as a team member, your dissenting views need to remain unspoken once the decision has been made.

Being part of a team also offers a sense of camaraderie and support. It is exhilarating to be valued for your unique contributions and to work with other talented experts. For me and for many of the women in my seminars, this is one of the best parts of the jump.

Questions to Consider. How important is autonomy to you? Are you prepared to spend more time on campus and to have less control over your time? Can you imagine yourself as a member of a team? What would you enjoy about being part of a team?

From a Shared Path to Individual Ambition

Making the jump requires acknowledging the power of your own ambition. You need to have the confidence that you are prepared for the job and the resilience to survive scrutiny and rejection. I see many women holding themselves back because of a lack of confidence in their abilities or because of the challenge of managing the negative feelings of applying for and then not getting the job. I see others give up after the first or second rejection, finding it too difficult to put themselves on the line again.

As a senior leader, you have to chart your own professional path. Unlike the regularly timed stages of progression as a faculty member— from assistant to associate to full professor—or the progression from assistant coach to coach, administrative careers often zig and zag. You will likely be faced with a range of positions available and will have to make decisions about what to do next and when. This can be overwhelming but also liberating.

Questions to Consider. Are you comfortable owning your ambition? Do you have a sense of your ultimate career goal? Could you handle publicly wanting a job and not getting it? What would it feel like to face rejection or failure? Are you ready to take that risk?

From Expert to Generalist

If you are a professor, your entire career path has likely been devoted to becoming an expert in a specific, relatively narrow domain. Your professional confidence and identity are tied to this expertise. It undergirds your research and determines the kind of upper-level or graduate courses you teach. You may also teach a general survey course, but even that is more or less confined to a particular field that you have studied for many years.

Becoming a full-time leader means losing the comfort of expertise and embracing a more fluid way of knowing, grounded in experience as well as research. As a dean, vice president, or president, doing lots of things well is more important than knowing everything about one thing. You will move from a budget meeting, to a personnel decision, to giving a speech in rapid succession. A broad grasp of multiple topics is required along with the ability to quickly synthesize new information.

If you are used to the leisurely pace of discovery that accompanies academic research, the rapid decision-making that is part of these senior roles can feel like a roller coaster. As urgent problems arise, there is rarely time to research the situation as fully as you would if you were writing an academic paper about it. Many decisions require assumptions about variables that can't be known.

Being a generalist can be deeply satisfying in that you are able to make use of a wide variety of skills and information. One vice president described how great it felt to be able to put her experience to good use in so many areas ("grant writing, general education and assessment, faculty development, donor relations, strategic planning"). She noted that this breadth allowed her to ask good questions and make better decisions.

Questions to Consider. Can you embrace a fluid approach to knowing and understanding? How much information do you need in order to make a decision? When are you comfortable relying on the expertise of others? Are you curious about the skills needed to be a good leader and willing to learn?

From Colleague to Employee

If you have been a faculty member, the jump may mark the first time you have had a clearly defined boss. Unlike a department chair, your boss has a great deal of say over how you spend your time and what projects you take on. Since you are no longer governed under the faculty handbook, your boss likely has more discretion in your evaluation and compensation. She can definitely fire you—or at least remove you from your administrative post. But she should also be there to support you, advise you, mentor you, and take the heat on your behalf.

Your boss will expect you to give her frank advice as she makes decisions. Once she has decided, she will expect you to loyally implement her plan. Obviously, if your boss makes a decision that you think is unethical or truly disastrous, you have the option to take a forceful stand, or even resign. But outside of these extremes, you are expected to have her back and vocally champion her agenda.

Questions to Consider. Will you be able to loyally support a boss and contribute to her goals? What kinds of things would be impossible for you to support? How would you handle a disagreement with your boss? What might you like about having a boss? What might feel confining?

For some of you, the jump marks the first time you have ever been someone else's boss. You now have the complex responsibility to support and guide people whose livelihood depends on your approval. You have to delegate and provide the right measure of support even as you allow someone else to tackle the problem. You hire and—very difficult—sometimes have to fire.

As the boss of others you are responsible for managing boundaries. You need to remain aware that your employees recognize the power dynamic at play. Your friendly invitation to see a movie will be interpreted as a can't-miss event. The formality and distance that have to be maintained in this context can be difficult for women who are used to building networks of friends at work.

Questions to Consider. What makes for a good boss? How do I plan to give feedback? How comfortable am I with delegating? Am I at risk of micromanaging? How can I draw comfortable boundaries while still being supportive and friendly?

Transitions at Any Career Stage

Transitions, of course, continue throughout your career. They often become more intense as you reach senior levels of responsibility.

From Individual to Symbol

Many senior leadership roles include an expectation that you will serve as a symbol of the institution. Your presence at events, such as graduation or convocation, signifies the sanctity of these occasions. Your presence at lectures, presentations, athletic contests, and cultural events is taken as a sign that the institution values them. You will likely also be asked to publicly represent the institution at external events.

It can be disorienting to be treated as a symbol. Not only does it keep you busy—there are lots of occasions that require your attendance—

but you have to subsume part of your own identity into the role. You may not have as much time for the campus events you enjoy attending because you have to spread yourself around. You also have to be aware that others will be watching you and noting your level of engagement and enthusiasm.

The symbolism, however, is an important form of power, and you can use it to highlight issues and people about whom you feel strongly. Your interest in them signals that they are important to the institution as a whole.

Questions to Consider. Am I comfortable subordinating my individual identity to my symbolic role? How do I feel about the symbolic rituals of higher education? How can I use my symbolic role to bring attention to important aspects of my institution?

From Earner to Breadwinner

Senior administrative roles typically pay better than the job you were doing before you made the jump. The higher salary recognizes the increased level of responsibility, the 24/7 nature of the role, and the relative scarcity of effective candidates. While more money should feel like a positive thing, it can sometimes be a source of ambivalence and anxiety for women.

The prospect of a sudden leap in salary brings into relief a woman's often-unconscious beliefs about money. Some women discover that they don't believe they deserve a high salary, or they equate a certain income level with behaviors or traits they don't respect. Others find that they are too ready to equate salary with personal worth and are in danger of taking a job that pays well but might not be right for them in other ways. Since salaries are expressed by specific numbers, they easily lend themselves to score-keeping.

Sometimes, a new salary can generate feelings of guilt. One provost noted, "When you have viewed yourself as an advocate for the underrepresented for so much of your life, and all of a sudden you find yourself with an income that is three times that of a hardworking staff member, that can make you feel that when you continue to publicly advocate for the ideals in the way you used to, you may be perceived as hypocritical."

Sometimes, relationship problems arise for women who find themselves out-earning their partner. Not every woman or couple finds this to be a problem, but cultural norms can creep into your brain when you least expect them. Many women are embarrassed to discover that they or their partner have latent, sometimes unconscious feelings about who should be earning more money. These concerns can be especially acute if your new job requires a move and your partner has to leave their own job in order to accompany you. The new weight of being the main or sole breadwinner can be surprisingly stressful.

A higher salary can also put additional pressure on you to demonstrate your value or, as one woman in a seminar put it, "to publicly perform your hard work to demonstrate that you are worth the high salary." This can lead to burnout as you forgo rest, relaxation, and even sleep.

Questions to Consider. What did money mean in your family as you were growing up? What would it feel like to earn more than your partner? Than your father or mother? How do you see the relationship between money and security? Between money and self-worth? What will you do with more money? How will you spend or save it? With whom are you comfortable talking about money? What would you never trade for money?

From Dressing for Yourself to Executive Style

The question of what to wear as a leader is serious for women. Men in leadership don't have to give much thought to their personal style. They wear a suit. They decide whether they want to wear a regular tie or a bow tie—bow-tie-wearing presidents are a distinct type—and then they stick with that day after day. For casual occasions, they put on khaki pants, a golf shirt, and possibly a sport coat. No one notices or cares if they are wearing the same suit or pants to every event. No one comments on their clothes. And unless they have a truly unusual hairstyle or some other distinguishing feature, no one comments on their personal appearance.

Women leaders, however, are under constant scrutiny. Everything from your nails to your lipstick to your weight to your hair to your wardrobe will be regularly noticed and evaluated. The newspaper will describe you in terms of your age and your clothes. A donor will ask where you bought your shoes. Your vice president might remind you that you have worn that same dress in recent photographs and thus need an alternative. As with women politicians, you will be critiqued for being too attractive or not attractive enough. One of my friends was sent to a stylist by the board that hired her. Another was told she should always wear earrings. In both cases, the intention was to be helpful. The board members wanted these women to succeed, and they were realistic about the fact that a polished appearance is important for a woman's credibility.

This kind of scrutiny and the need to develop a professional style that passes muster are daunting but come with the job. The good news is that within the overall imperative to be polished and well put together, there is a wide range of acceptable styles. There is a lot of room for variety and for putting forward your personal sense of style and self-presentation. The women presidents I know look very different from one another, but they all look terrific.

As long as you dress as though you thought about what you are wearing and put an outfit together with intention and care, and as long as you are neat, age-appropriate, and wearing clothes that fit well and that trusted friends would deem "professional," you can pretty much wear any style you want. For the most part, this flexibility extends to a multiplicity of styles for women of all ethnicities. I have seen successful women leaders in higher education wear afros, dreadlocks, hijabs, sheitels, and saris. At the highest levels, I don't see visible tattoos, piercings, or multicolored hair. But even that may change as the next generation of leaders emerges.

Questions to Consider. Are you comfortable with your professional style? Are you prepared to be scrutinized? In your view, what is "executive" attire for women? Could you imagine being on a campus with a very formal culture? A very informal culture? Are you prepared for the time and expense required to appear polished on a daily basis?

From "Front of the House" to "Back of the House"

Even as your appearance is being scrutinized, you might feel more invisible as a senior administrator than you did as a professor or lower-level administrator. As a faculty member, you were used to your name being on the publication and listed as the instructor for your courses. Most institutions offer awards for teaching and for research, and you were able to talk publicly about your work and its consequences. As an entry-level administrator, you were used to regular, positive feedback and engagement with students. You could point to specific accomplishments and have them publicly recognized.

As a senior administrator, a lot of your work is devoted to helping others achieve their goals. You are likely to be working behind the scenes. Because your effort often involves resolving personnel issues, much of it has to remain confidential. I am not aware of any institution that gives an award for great deaning! Moreover, you are often managing ongoing problems rather than resolving them once and for all. That can make it difficult to find a sense of closure and achievement.

One associate vice president noted, "For the first few years I would come home every night and think, 'What did I accomplish today?' You are used to being focused on a set of deliverables and a checklist (run through this program, teach this class, and so on) [and] the[n] your whole world shifts to hour-by-hour changes. . . . It can be hard to navigate when considering your output, value, and worth on a day-to-day basis."

Questions to Consider. How will I feel when others get credit for my work? Can I tolerate a more ambiguous sense of success? Am I comfortable with confidentiality?

As a professor or more junior administrator, you have the support and comfort that comes with being part of a faculty or department. You likely have an overall esprit de corps and a sense of solidarity with your peers. You might even define yourself partly in terms of your membership in this group and in distinction from others on campus, for example, administrators, "suits," staff, students.

The moment you become a senior administrator, you lose this status. No matter how long or how well you served as a member of the faculty or administrative department, your new role immediately marks you as "other." It can be shocking to see how quickly this happens. Your colleagues may couch this in jokes about you going over to the dark side or becoming a suit, but they are serious. They are letting you know that you are no longer welcome in the "we" of the faculty or the department.

In your new role, your closest colleagues are your senior administrative peers. This is a much smaller group, and depending on your position and the size of the institution, you may not have any exact peers. This is one reason being an administrator can be lonely. As a professor, you could commiserate with hundreds of other faculty members about the stress of grading or preparing a class. But as a dean, there won't be many people on campus who truly understand your work or with whom you can trade stories and support.

You are also likely to find that you have fewer women peers—and even fewer of them will be women of color or queer women—the higher you rise, and this can exacerbate the sense of isolation. Seeing your former friends subtly exclude you from the lunch table or the after-work drink can bring back memories of the mean girls from junior high. Being able to understand and accept that you are not going to be seen as one of the pack will help you keep from taking this personally. It is also important to find friends beyond campus with whom you can share the stresses and joys of your work. One new dean told me that she found support through an online community of women of color in similar roles. Others have mentioned the American Conference of Academic Deans, the American Council on Education, the Council of Independent Colleges, and the Association of American Colleges and Universities as providing important networking opportunities.

Questions to Consider. Am I prepared for the change in my relationship with colleagues? In my new role, will I be the only woman or the only woman of color? How have I dealt with feeling left out in the past? Where will I draw support from? What kind of new relationships would I like to make?

Presidential Transitions

The presidency is unlike any other campus role. Many of the transitions discussed above are magnified. You are more of a symbol, your clothes and style are more significant, and you are even more of a generalist. But there are additional unique transitions that the presidency requires.

From Having a Boss to Reporting to a Board

As a president, you no longer report to an individual; you report to a board of trustees. This is one of the biggest changes that the role brings. There is nothing in your previous career that prepares you for this new reporting relationship. It is unique and somewhat odd. Everyone—and no one—is your boss. Your board will look to you for leadership and direction even as you look to the members for support and guidance. The board will have its own internal politics and practices that you will have to understand and navigate. Learning to work effectively with the board is essential for a successful presidency. For an outstanding overview of this issue, I recommend Susan Resneck Pierce's chapter "The President and the Board" in her book *On Being Presidential.*[2]

Questions to Consider. Am I prepared for the ambiguity of reporting to a board? How will I build relationships with individual trustees and with the board as a whole? What kind of support do I need from the board?

From One among Many to Sui Generis

As the president, you have no campus peer. Your duties, responsibilities, and pressures are yours alone. It can make the job very lonely. It is important to build a support network of external colleagues to whom you can turn for advice and friendship. Involvement in national organizations and regional consortia is a great way to meet other women college presidents. I have found a lively and collegial rapport with many of them. Your family and friends will need to understand the demands of your job and enough about higher ed that they can offer meaningful advice and consolation. Many presidents also work with an executive coach. This is something boards are usually willing to pay for if you request it. The more people on your team, the better.

Questions to Consider. How will I build a support network? What organizations can I join that will connect me to other women leaders?

From Private Citizen to Public Figure

As the president of a college or university, you are considered a public figure. While the scope of your influence varies with the size and prominence of your institution, there is no way to escape this part of the job entirely.

As a public figure, your opinion will be sought, your presence will be requested at community events, and the local newspaper (and, in some cases, the national news) will write about you. Invitations will pour in, and you will need to be thoughtful about how you spend your time and with whom you share your messages.

As a woman, the pressures can be even more complex. Early in my first presidency, I learned that there was some community criticism about the fact that I had not joined the boards of some of the key women's service organizations in town. When I asked my supportive advisors about this, I learned that for generations, the wife of the college president had been active in these groups. The members thus expected that I would be too—forgetting that as the president and not the presidential spouse I wouldn't have much time for this kind of thing. I was fortunate to have some wonderful local friends—some of them wives of trustees—who gently redirected the town's expectations on my behalf.

It is important to have staff members who can advise you. At a minimum, you should have an experienced communications director with media experience and a community relations expert as part of your team. Ask for professional advice or training if you have to do television interviews or engage in other media appearances.

I learned the hard way that women need to be thoughtful about being photographed since it can be a challenge to convey the requisite presidential demeanor and at the same time meet the expectation that a woman should look friendly. The first set of official photos turned out to be unusable since in my attempt to follow the photographer's instruction to look relaxed by leaning against a pillar, I wound up looking too casual and even—in some of the shots—sort of "come hither." That is not the effect for which we were aiming.

Look at photos of other women presidents to help you decide on poses and settings that will work for you. Consider getting professional makeup and hairstyling before a photo shoot. Be frank with the photographer about what you want to convey. And ask a trusted friend or colleague to review the photos to make sure they don't look too distracting, unprofessional, or severe.

Questions to Consider. Am I comfortable being interviewed by reporters? How can I improve my media skills? What visual image do I want to convey in professional photographs? Who will advise me in this?

From a Job to a Lifestyle

The presidency is a 24/7 commitment. There are expectations about the involvement of your family, about where and how you will make a home, and about your availability. You wind up being extremely visible. Your alumni and their families are everywhere, and they have seen your picture and read about your appointment. They will recognize you when they see you.

Even though I have only ever worked at small colleges, I have been recognized in foreign countries, on the beach, in small towns, and in large cities. I assume that every time I get on a plane, someone will ask, "Aren't you the president of my college?" I never count on anonymity, which means that there is a sense in which I am always at work.

I've lived in a college-owned house for almost twenty years. So even our family home is connected to my job. Our children grew up knowing that there would be regular receptions and dinner parties. Our policy was that they were rarely required to attend, but they were always welcome. They could wear whatever they wanted since it was their house. They made varied choices depending on their age and their unique personality. But each of our children has grown up to be comfortable in a variety of social situations and understands the importance of making guests feel welcome.

My husband is a great host and an asset for me in my role as a provost and now as a president. Together, we have developed strategies to make sure that we meet the public obligations of my work while still having a private life for our family.

Questions to Consider. Am I ready to be on stage much of the time? How will I carve out some privacy? Is my family prepared for the changes a presidency brings? What role will my partner play?

Putting It into Practice

Naming and reflecting on these transitions is a way of preparing for the next step in your career. Ideally, this self-examination will help you recognize some of the ambivalent feelings that might arise and leave you better prepared to manage the initial sense of dislocation that accompanies the jump.

There is an exciting future on the other side of these transitions. You will be in a position to make good on your initial motivations. You will have the opportunity to serve students by improving their academic and co-curricular experiences. You will have the opportunity to serve faculty and staff by creating a more just work environment.

And you will have the opportunity to serve the world by building educational institutions that produce graduates with the skills and the passion to tackle the world's most pressing problems.

Your leadership matters.

2

Navigating Power and Conflict

———

I WAS APPOINTED as provost in the same semester that I was scheduled to stand for promotion to full professor. I assumed that this would not be an issue. I was a well-respected faculty member of long standing and had met the department's and the college's standards for service, scholarship, and teaching. Since the tenure and promotion committee usually sent its recommendations to the provost, the president and I agreed that the recommendation in my case would go directly to him. He would then continue the process as usual, making a decision and bringing that to the board for confirmation. Naïvely, I assumed that this workaround would be enough to allay any faculty concerns.

But I soon found that my appointment as provost made me an object of suspicion to some of my faculty colleagues. Members of the faculty governance committee worried that the tenure committee would feel pressured to approve my case lest I somehow use my new power to retaliate against them. They demanded to bring this issue before the faculty. I was stunned. These were people who had worked with me for more than a decade and who, I thought, knew me as a person of fairness and integrity. I didn't believe they could suddenly imagine me to be a vindictive ogre. I was fortunate that the faculty as a whole agreed that the workaround was fine, and the process could move forward.

This was an extremely painful episode for me. In the midst of it, I called my father for advice. Not only is he a psychoanalyst but he had once served as the dean of the school of the Chicago Psychoanalytic Institute, so I knew his advice would be grounded in both psychological insight and experience. He was not surprised that there was an aura of suspicion and anxiety around my promotion case. But he told me that it had nothing to do with me personally. My new role meant that lots of people would be interacting with me through the lens of their unconscious beliefs about power. Some people think power is to be resisted. Others think it is to be seduced. Still others think it is to be supported or negotiated with. The way people would engage with me would often be shaped by these unconscious beliefs. I needed to learn not to take this personally. Power and conflict would now be an ordinary part of my working life and would need to be managed in a variety of ways.

I was surprised by the emphasis he placed on power as a definitive part of my work as provost. I had been thinking about the responsibilities that came with this new position, but I was reluctant to acknowledge that my new role was a powerful one. It made me uncomfortable to think about this—as though suddenly I had become a tyrant or a dictator.

It helped to remember that power is structural. Like privilege, it can't simply be denounced or set aside. To pretend that I didn't have power within my institutional structure was disingenuous. It was equally wrong to imagine that I held power in some absolute sense. My new job title gave me lots of authority. But I wielded that power in a context that allowed for multiple forms of agency, resistance, and action.

Power in the Academy

The academic power complex includes formal roles for shared governance and faculty authority in areas of curriculum development and tenure. It also includes multiple forms of soft power as individuals form coalitions, build consensus, foment resistance, or take action. The values of each institution determine how soft power is distributed. At a research university, the most powerful faculty member might be the one who attracts the most funding or has garnered the most prestigious external awards. At a liberal arts college, power might accrue to the faculty member who has the best reputation as a teacher and mentor and has built up a cadre of loyal almuni. In every context, though, power is enhanced through the formation of relationships and the ability to deploy those relationships in the service of a desired outcome.

Unlike in a corporate environment, power in a college or university is top-down, bottom-up, and even side-to-side. Change might be as likely to happen as a result of a student protest as by a formal vote of the faculty senate. The organizational chart might put the president at the top, but the football coach may have more practical power. The board might be in the sway of a donor or legislator. I know of one campus where the admission dean had significant power: every decision involved his perspective, and even the president bent to his judgment. On another campus, a long-serving housekeeper had the power to activate student, staff, and faculty support to save the jobs of some of her co-workers during a reduction in staff.

As a woman, even a high-level title might not signal your power to others. In my first presidency, I was regularly asked what role my male predecessor was playing at the college now. Often, the questioner assumed that the former president was now the chancellor or the chair of the board. They knew I was the president, but they couldn't quite believe that I was really in charge. The real (male) president had to be somewhere in the wings overseeing my work.

You too will likely encounter patriarchal assumptions and attitudes. There will be donors who want a man in the room if a major gift is under discussion. Alumni will want to test whether you can "take" a sexist joke. You will be introduced and written about with references to your age, your style, and your status as a mother or wife. Your attractiveness will be commented on. (I often hear that I am too pretty to be a college president; no doubt, at some point I will be considered too old or too haggard to be one.) It might be assumed that you will automatically side with women and be too "personally" involved to set fair policies and processes around Title IX issues or other gender-based discrimination.

There are multiple ways to respond to these provocations: humor, a frank rebuttal, changing the subject, subtle renunciation. You will have to decide which battles are worth fighting and which to let go—both on your own behalf and on behalf of other women. My own style is to accept what seems to be meant in good cheer with a gentle reframing and to save more direct or confrontational responses for situations in which genuine hostility seems to be at play.

Even admitting that these encounters happen at all can be difficult because women leaders worry that they reveal our weaknesses. In her essay "Madame President: Gender's Impact in the Presidential Suite," Mary L. Bucklin notes: "Although the [women] presidents are clearly aware of the role that gender played in their leadership experiences, they seemed to be hesitant to describe situations that showed its impact on them. . . . Several of the participants chose to communicate concerns about the gender dynamics of being in top-level leadership by sharing stories of situations other women presidents had faced."[1]

I empathize with this reluctance. I rarely speak publicly about the more egregious and embarrassing forms sexism has taken in my career because I worry that those stories would undermine my credibility. But I also work toward greater courage. Keeping our stories of sexism to ourselves reinforces the idea that they arise because of our individual failings. Sharing them gives them their rightful place as symptoms of broader patriarchal structures.

As women, we need to cultivate toughness and resiliency at the same time as we acknowledge our vulnerabilities. Claiming our power in the face of resistance is a sign of our strength. Learning to understand and use my own power continues to be a journey for me.

One practice that I have found helpful is to begin with an inventory of my formal responsibilities and the resources that are under my authority. Your list might include the power to make personnel decisions, the power to add or subtract resources from projects and departments, the power to tell the story of your institution, the power to frame debates, the power to set priorities, and on and on. I then consider the various constraints on these forms of formal power. According to the formal governance structure, who needs to be consulted? Who needs to approve? Who needs to agree? And—equally important—based on the informal structure of relationships and authority within the institution, who needs to be on board?

Paying attention to the formal structure and ignoring the informal one is a common rookie mistake. It is easy to see why: understanding the informal network and structure takes time and immersion in the day-to-day life of the institution. A newcomer won't have the requisite knowledge or wisdom until she has listened, learned, and observed. Seeking to understand these relations is one of the key tasks for your first year in a new institution.

Your formal power will be enhanced—and you will be more likely to use it wisely—if you take the time to build relationships. Knowing and understanding the institution from as many perspectives as you possibly can are crucial to good leadership. These insights will help you decide what has to be done and will help you actually do it.

One of my first experiences in leadership happened just after I received tenure. I was asked to direct Muhlenberg College's Center for Ethics, which didn't have a physical location or any staff. It was not much more than a framework for coordinating campus-wide programming and lectures. I knew these programs wouldn't succeed without the active engagement of faculty members who would link the center's programs to their classes, encourage students to attend, and share their expertise and contacts with me.

Since I didn't have any designated faculty lines or structural authority to compel participation, I soon learned that using my modest budget to create opportunities for informal faculty gatherings and conversations was my most effective tool. Faculty members enjoyed talking with their colleagues, and they enjoyed developing and taking ownership of programming that interested them. I joked that the essence of my power as the center's director was my ability to deploy the "wine-and-cheese budget." But this is a joke grounded in a deep truth. Using your resources to create meaningful opportunities for others will strengthen the power of your own projects. Now, when I advise others to make good use of their wine-and-cheese budget, I mean that they should look for opportunities to draw faculty or staff together for informal conversations about important issues. In these settings, good ideas emerge, coalitions form, and a leader can both listen and speak—often more frankly than in a formal meeting.

Both formal and relational power are shaped by the power of your character. In their book *Women at the Top: What Women University and College Presidents Say about Effective Leadership*, Mimi Wolverton, Beverly L. Bower, and Adrienne E. Hyle interviewed Betty L. Siegel, former president of Kennesaw State University. Siegel emphasizes that the power that comes from your inner strength is of particular value:

> Power is not a position. Now there is a lot that goes with the position of president. I can make things happen. But those things are minute compared to what can be done through personal power. To me, personal power is Cyrano de Bergerac's "white plume" of leadership, the authenticity of the leader, the attitudes, beliefs, and values which you hold true. We ought to aspire to that, not to power. The perks of power leave with the job. The personal power you develop doesn't leave you.[2]

In addition to your actual power, you also have perceived power. Others will see you as more powerful than you feel and more powerful than you really are. They may imagine that the powers you wield are limitless, forgetting how many actual constraints there are on your decisions. Your perceived power changes the ways people relate to you. As my father's advice reminded me, this isn't something you can change or wish away. Asking people to set aside their perception about power won't be seen as kind or humble—more likely, it will be seen as false or manipulative. This was true when I was a dean and is even more true now that I am a president.

In practice, this means I am respectful of the ways that people perceive my power. I am cautious about blurring the line between colleague and friend. I accept Facebook friend requests from colleagues, but I don't initiate them. I remind myself that it is hard to say no to the president, and so I try not to ask for things that go beyond the professional. I am aware as well that others sometimes hold back from inviting me to socialize because they don't want to look as though they are overstepping a boundary or kissing up. Senior leadership roles can be lonely so it is important to cultivate relationships outside your institution or with colleagues who are in peer positions.

Many of the transitions discussed in chapter 1 have their origins in the actual or perceived power imbalance that appears after you make the jump. As my father noted, the filter through which your colleagues interact with you has been altered.

Using your power wisely is the essence of good leadership, and I discuss this in detail in chapter 4, "Growing as a Leader." I find it helpful to conceive of my authority as the "power to" accomplish goals rather than the "power over" individuals. This keeps me focused on the institution and reminds me that the resources under my control are not really mine. I am a steward of the institutional budget and mission. Every decision has to be for the greater good.

This perspective allows me to take on the tough responsibilities that come with power. For example, continuing to employ someone who is doing a poor job simply because I like them would be fine if I were paying them with my own money. But the institution's money isn't mine. Every dollar I spend was given to the college by students or on behalf of students. I have to make certain that I am using that money in ways that provide the absolute best learning environment possible. It isn't right to let my personal feelings subvert that goal. Stating this explicitly to myself and to my cabinet helps us remain focused on our responsibility to make difficult decisions with as much wisdom as we can muster.

Clarity in Communication

The fact that you are in a powerful position means that you have to be especially careful to make your communication clear and direct. A university president was once astonished to discover that some of the faculty assumed he had green-lighted an expensive building project. Their reasoning: when they discussed it with him, he had been friendly and hadn't explicitly said no. He "didn't blink" when they mentioned the price. They took this as a yes. His story underscores for me how important it is to give clear signals about where you stand when something is proposed.

It is okay to say maybe as long as you truly mean it. Using "maybe" as a friendly way of saying no, however, is not effective. When I do say maybe, I try to give a sense of the conditions that would need to occur before I would be able to say yes (e.g., "we would need to have a budget surplus," or "we would need to find donor support for this," or " it would need to be approved by the curriculum committee"). If I can't think of a scenario that would make it possible to say yes, then it is usually better to say no.

Don't be afraid to say that you can't even commit to a maybe until you have thought about it or have gotten more information. I learned the hard way that I make better decisions if I wait to make them until after the requester has left my office. This gives me a chance to reflect, perhaps ask for advice, and then give a more thoughtful response.

The need to be direct and firm is sometimes difficult for women. We are socialized to want to be liked and to build relationships. We know that our firmness can be misinterpreted as unfriendliness or worse. Many of us are used to dealing with our children where sometimes "maybe" is a useful way of changing the subject or interrupting a tantrum. But as leaders, we can't equivocate or send mixed signals. We have to say yes, no, and maybe with conviction. Saying no to someone you like is hard. Saying yes to someone you don't like is also hard. But both of these responses are sometimes in the institution's best interests, and you have to be tough enough to make these choices.

Part of leadership is having to convey news to others that may disappoint or anger them. Letting someone know that they didn't get the job or award, that their performance is problematic, or even worse, that they are being fired is one of the hardest parts of my job.

If the conversation has legal implications, I recommend having another person in the room besides you and the staff or faculty member to whom you are responding. The human resources director is often ideal. She can take notes, make sure that you are not putting the college at risk, and also continue the conversation with the person by giving them a sense of next steps. The initial meeting should be direct and brief. If a longer discussion about the future is necessary, that is usually best reserved for another day.

When the person arrives for the meeting at which I have to deliver bad news, I generally start with a gentle warning: "I am about to tell you something that might be difficult to hear," or "we need to have a difficult conversation." This alerts the person and gives them a moment to prepare. Then I just say the hard thing directly: "I have serious concerns about how you are doing your job," or "I can't continue you in this position," or "the search committee has gone in a different direction," or "your appeal was rejected." Being direct may seem harsh, but I think it is important that there be no ambiguity. The other person should not have to guess what I am trying to say.

After I have clearly delivered the verdict, I then go back and say something about what led to this decision. If there is an appeal process—as there might be in a negative tenure decision, for example—I briefly explain that option. I usually suggest that the person take some time to absorb the news and then if they want to pursue an appeal we can discuss the details in a few days. When someone has had a shock, they don't always take in all the information so be prepared to review the content of the conversation after the person has internalized the news.

In that initial meeting, I do not get into a debate about whether the decision is fair or not. I suggest that the person take some time to organize their thoughts and then we can discuss the situation at a later date if necessary. At this point, it is more important to make sure the person understands that a decision has been made and briefly why. You can let the person explain their objection, but trying to respond to their points is unlikely to be effective. Rather than arguing, I find it is better to say something more general: "I understand you do not agree," or "I appreciate that you have an alternative perspective on this."

One of the biggest mistakes that some leaders make is covering their discomfort at having to deliver bad news with anger. They get irritated or defensive when the other person pushes back and is angry or upset. This is unproductive. Of course, the person is mad at you. Of course, they are feeling strong negative emotions. Of course, they feel the process was unfair. You are not going to convince them they should feel differently. It is best to just acknowledge their feeling ("I understand this makes you angry") and then reiterate calmly that the situation is final ("but the decision has been made").

Another mistake is to think you can be both executioner and comforter. If you have just delivered hard news to someone, you can be compassionate and kind, but you can't be the one to help them process their feelings or cajole them into looking on the bright side. It is awful to have to be the bad guy. For women, who are socialized to always want to be liked, the knowledge that we are the villain in someone else's story can be tough to take. It is natural to want to rebuild a relationship that feels as though it has just been severed. But power differentials have to be acknowledged. You have the power to fire this person or to make a negative judgment that has impacted their career. You are not able to play the role of supportive friend.

That doesn't mean you can't assist them in finding support. If there are resources that my college can offer, I share those. If I believe I can serve as a positive reference for the person in the future, I mention that. I often call the college chaplain and let them know that someone has just received bad news. The chaplain can then check in and offer comfort. The human resources office can also be called on to offer information about next steps and to answer questions.

Managing Conflict

It is almost a law of nature that power breeds resistance and conflict. You may be wielding your power with perfect justice and wisdom, but people will still disagree with you and even resent you. Knowing how to manage resistance and conflict is one of the most important skills a leader can develop. In my seminars, the session on conflict management is often the most lively and ultimately the most useful for participants.

When we get to this topic, there is always nervous laughter. I remind everyone that we will learn more if we share our experiences honestly. And then I tell a story or two about my own difficulties with conflict. I describe the angry mother who mocked me on the phone; the staff member who had to be escorted off campus because they were threatening violence; or the long-standing departmental feud that only got worse when I tried to "fix" it. One by one, the participants tell stories of their own. A dean was afraid to meet with a faculty member who had a reputation for shouting. Another, longer-serving dean was surprised to discover that she had developed a reputation for being mean: what she saw as firmness, others interpreted as anger. A provost reported that she was running herself ragged trying to engage with disaffected faculty members.

Most of us learned our conflict management styles as children. Unless you have spent focused time relearning, whatever you adopted at home is still likely your go-to strategy. Understanding these styles is an important step in developing your ability to manage conflict effectively. One widely used and helpful taxonomy is the Thomas-Kilmann model, which identifies five basic conflict styles:

> *accommodators*, whose first impulse is to yield and let the other
> person's view take center stage
> *avoiders*, who use hiding, delay, or distraction to avoid having to
> deal with conflict openly
> *compromisers*, who look to find a solution that is in the middle of
> two divergent viewpoints
> *collaborators*, who want to work with the other person to find a
> win-win or mutually acceptable solution
> *competitors*, who refuse to yield ground and want to see that they
> win and the other person loses[3]

You probably identify with one or more of these strategies. It usually isn't hard to figure out which were prevalent in your family and which serve as your usual response when you are challenged or otherwise drawn into a conflict. Reflecting on your own conflict history deepens your self-understanding. Ideally, you can use this awareness to provide more freedom for yourself by learning how to effectively use each of the styles rather than being trapped by your habits.

In my view, the best leaders are adept at all of these styles and can make a conscious choice to adopt a particular approach based on the situation at hand. There are instances, for example, when avoidance is actually the best strategy. Sometimes, putting off the argument gives everyone time to calm down. Sometimes, the problem even resolves itself. But using avoidance in every situation is likely unwise. So too with the other styles. They each have a place in your leadership repertoire. There isn't a single style that is always best or always bad. The trouble comes when you only have one kind of response, and it becomes your default.

Even the competitor style has its time and place. As women, we can expect to encounter situations in which our authority is being intentionally undermined. When this occurs and you are aware that you are being challenged by someone who is not looking for a solution to a problem but is seeking to "put you in your place," an outright assertion of your authority is appropriate. Sometimes, the best answer is what we say to our children when the time for argument and discussion is over: "because I said so." Just as it would be a serious mistake to make competition your primary conflict management style, it would equally be a mistake to be afraid to use it when necessary.

I recommend looking at the list of styles and thinking about which you employ and which you never employ. You can spend some time identifying the kind of situation that would call for each of the styles. If there are some that you never use, you might consider practicing them. The more free you are to choose an appropriate response to a given situation and the more tools you have at your disposal, the better you will be able to resolve conflicts as they arise.

Polarities versus Problems

Polarity thinking offers another helpful model for framing the challenges at your college. As a leader, the list of problems facing your institution might seem endless. Often, what seem like problems on college campuses turn out to be polarities. A "polarity" has been defined as tension between mutually important and reinforcing values.[4]

A common polarity arises in debates about the curriculum where one faction argues in favor of greater breadth and the other insists on depth. Breadth and depth reinforce one another—the broader your general knowledge, the more you understand the context for your specialization; and the deeper your expertise, the better you can appreciate your field's applications to a wider set of problems and issues. Both breadth and depth are important, and curricular debates won't settle the balance once and for all. Breadth versus depth isn't a problem to be solved, it is a polarity to be managed.

The most emotionally charged and seemingly intractable issues on college campuses often reveal underlying polarities. The clash between the value of freedom of expression and the value of respect for all people is one example. Another is the conflict that arises between the value of believing and supporting victims of sexual assault and the value of ensuring fair and impartial treatment for those accused. In cases like these, we can affirm the importance of the values held by both sides of the debate even as we seek to resolve the tensions between them.

Recognizing a polarity allows you to look for solutions that balance the competing values, help both sides appreciate the perspective of the other, and recognize that a single, simple solution will not erase the need for ongoing management of the conflict.

When you are in charge of managing a resolution to a complex disagreement, see if you can reframe it as a polarity rather than a problem. This can have the effect of reducing the emotional tenor of the debate and offering terms that can suggest compromise.

Difficult Feelings

In order to manage conflict well, you have to be able to tolerate someone else's negative feelings. Early in my leadership career, I realized that I was working very hard to avoid making the men with whom I worked angry. I would tiptoe around, avoid, and try to manage the situation so that I wouldn't experience a man's strong emotions.

There are good reasons for women to fear men's anger and to be aware that male violence is a possibility. But my specific worries weren't grounded in a belief that the men with whom I worked would lash out at me physically. It was a more general sense that part of my role as a woman was to manage men's emotions and court their good opinion. Once I saw and named this pattern, it became easier for me to change it. I learned to separate actual threat from more abstract worry. Most important, I learned that I could tolerate a man's anger without feeling that I had to soothe it.

An African American woman who participated in one of my seminars noted that she had to fight against an ingrained sense that it was her job to manage and prevent the anger of white people. White anger is often a real danger to women of color, including when those white people have power over a woman's career. This woman's caution was sensible even though she recognized she needed to take more risks. Learning to let go of her default management of the feelings of white people was an important step in her development as a leader.

Some people—both men and women—use their own anger as a form of threat or coercion. They assume that others will accommodate them as soon as it becomes clear they might blow their top. But as you do with a toddler, you can make it clear that the tantrum doesn't affect you one way or another. You can coolly tell the person that you can't continue the conversation while they are shouting. They can come back later when they can discuss things calmly. If the anger is more subtle, you can say that you recognize that they are starting to feel strong emotions, and so you recommend taking a break and starting again tomorrow. Your ability to tolerate the anger of other people and to set clear limits undermines their ability to use their rising anger as a tool to coerce you.

Conflict management also requires us to tolerate our own anger and find ways of expressing it that move the situation forward. I have learned that as a college president even the slightest sign that I am annoyed is likely to get overinterpreted. A day after I send what I think of as a mildly displeased email, I am likely to hear that "everyone" heard that I was furious about something. If I ask a question in a meeting with any kind of sharpness in my voice, I see people visibly pull back or get immediately defensive. Anger is an area where power makes a difference. An angry subordinate can be dismissed, supported, or ignored, but an angry leader is perceived as a bully even when her anger is justified and appropriately expressed. Because this emotion is so potent, learning to manage your anger and the anger of people around you is an important leadership skill.

As women, we are often socialized to sublimate our anger or turn it inward, where it emerges as depression or anxiety. As I have gotten better at noticing the way anger feels in my body—for me, it is tightness in my belly and upper back—I have been better able to make use of it in ways that help me accomplish my goals.

I have also gotten better at figuring out what makes me angry. Sometimes, my anger is righteous, sparked by shoddy work or injustice. Sometimes, it is defensive, erupting in response to a real or perceived threat to me or to the college. Sometimes, it is simply a result of my impatience or a too tight schedule. Categorizing my anger often helps it dissipate. At the very least, it helps me respond more thoughtfully and effectively.

Even when we are comfortable with our own strong emotions, others may not be. In our patriarchal society, male anger is usually seen as powerful, but an angry woman is likely to be dismissed as hysterical or overly emotional. African American participants in my seminars have noted that this is even more of an issue for them. Being written off as an "angry Black woman" is deeply insulting, and the fear of being so labeled can inhibit expression of even the most warranted outrage. A Chinese colleague told me that her problem is the reverse. Her anger—no matter how explicit—is ignored because she is assumed to be docile and compliant. These stereotypes persist in many environments and are yet another hurdle for women of color. I encourage white women to take active responsibility for our internalized prejudices and learn to treat the anger of women of color with respect and acknowledgment.

Given the dismissive ways that women's anger is treated, it can be hard to find approaches to expressing your anger that empower rather than deplete you. It is unfair, but women are often taken more seriously when they express anger on behalf of others rather than on their own behalf. Finding ways to tie your anger to an issue that affects others may generate a more satisfying response. Expressing your anger calmly may also yield better results.

Being calm is not the same thing as denying your anger. Saying "I am not mad" when you clearly are is both disingenuous and personally demeaning. Better to say "I am feeling some anger about your response," or "this conversation is making me angry." As long as you can convey your feeling without shouting or belittling someone, acknowledging your own anger can serve as a sign of your authority and self-respect.

Tears are another aspect of strong emotions that interest the women in my seminars. I am not sure I know a woman who has never cried at work. Crying is a natural response to anger, disappointment, sadness, and frustration. The problem with crying is that it can be mistaken for weakness, and it plays into the stereotype of the overly emotional woman. If you find that tears well up in the midst of a tense conversation, a good way to handle this is to say something that reaffirms your strength and control of the situation. Possibilities include "don't mind my tears, I cry when I see an injustice," "crying is a way I respond when I am resolving a conflict," or "my practice is to cry for five minutes and then resume the conversation." Choose an approach that demonstrates that you are not ashamed about crying and that it hasn't derailed you or caused you to back away from the central points in the conversation.

You also sometimes have to deal with another person's tears. As with anger, it is important not to be coerced by someone else's strong feelings. You can be sympathetic and compassionate, but tears should not cause you to yield on an important point. I keep tissues in my office and have the box ready when I know a tough conversation will ensue. If someone cries, I reassure them that it is perfectly normal and that they are not the first person to cry in my office. I sometimes say "I've cried here too" to let them know that crying doesn't diminish them in my eyes. And I offer the person a chance to regroup and continue the conversation at a later point.

Managing Resistance

Resistance is unpleasant, but it is a necessary and even positive part of any institution. The women in my seminars sometimes are frustrated by trying to win over the most resistant faction. This is often a needless distraction. When they stop focusing on the "nevers," they find they have more time to spend with the "maybes." It is sometimes said that you should expect one-third of any group to be enthusiastic and supportive and one-third to be resistant. Hence the leader's job is to inspire and persuade the middle third. While this strikes me as an overly simplistic calculation, it is a good reminder: you will not be able to please everyone, but that doesn't mean that you are ineffective.

I also try to remember that the resisters often have a point, and listening to their perspective will help me make better decisions even if I can't get them fully on board. Moreover, many of the strongest naysayers on a campus are delightful individuals and fun to be with one-on-one. Sometimes, they are wonderful teachers or coaches and deeply committed to their work. I can put up with a lot of resistance when I know that students are being well served.

Resistance and conflict are not necessarily signs of disrespect. Someone can respect your autonomy, competence, and authority and still disagree with you or work against you. But as a woman leader, you are likely to occasionally encounter actual disrespect. Sometimes, the disrespect is overt, but more often it is covert. It can even come wrapped in a backhanded, pseudo compliment. You may feel insulted but not be able to pinpoint exactly why.

As I have tried to understand how covert disrespect works in my life and the lives of other women, I have realized that one source is the limited repertoire of cultural paradigms for how men and women relate to each other and the kinds of roles women play in a relationship. Instead of acknowledging a woman as a colleague, employee, or boss, some men—and even some women—revert to one or more of the standard and old-fashioned paradigms for interaction: woman as daughter, woman as mother, woman as wife.

In the daughter paradigm, you are treated as innocent, youthful, and in need of guidance. You are in this paradigm when you receive unasked-for advice from someone with demonstrably less experience and authority than you, when you receive mansplaining, or when someone offers you their unasked-for protection. You might receive a scolding if you are seen as ungrateful or disobedient. You might be offered pseudo compliments that emphasize the speaker's pleasant surprise at how well you are doing your job.

In the mother paradigm, you are seen as the source of soft authority—a rule-maker who can be wheedled out of her decisions or cajoled into overlooking bad behavior. You will recognize this one when you encounter surprise that you are enforcing a rule. Sulking and manipulation are also signs that someone is seeing you through this lens, as are attempts to appeal to a higher authority—a father figure—in order to overturn your decision or avoid recognizing your authority.

In the wife paradigm, you are assumed to be available to meet the emotional demands of others. There is an assumption that you are constantly available and ready to accommodate someone else's needs. You may be expected to soothe and manage their feelings. Demands and tantrums are signs that this paradigm is in play, as are requests for special attention or favoritism.

Recognizing when these paradigms are operating can help you understand why even compliments sometimes serve as signals of disrespect. It can also help you figure out how to resist others' attempts to subsume you under an outdated paradigm. And it may even help you realize the ways you too have internalized these paradigms and can fall into one or more of these familiar roles in your interactions with others.

Because these paradigms are unconscious, it can be difficult to avoid and respond to them. I sometimes use humor to reframe the underlying assumptions. Sometimes, I grit my teeth. And sometimes, I bring the underlying assumption to light ("I appreciate your advice, but this is an area in which I have a great deal of experience," or "I cannot treat you as special and bend the rule"). A new dean commented that it is extremely helpful to have a supervisor (or colleague) who recognizes these patterns as problematic and is willing to provide support as you set appropriate boundaries.

Putting It into Practice

As you learn more about your own relationship to power and your ability to manage conflict, you will find your interactions with others are more satisfying and productive.

Becoming an effective leader requires that you accept your own power and the resistance it generates. It also means expanding your repertoire of conflict management styles. Both power and conflict can be especially challenging for women because we are often socialized to acquiesce to the power of others. Taking on the responsibility of being a powerful woman leader requires ongoing learning and self-reflection.

REFLECTION QUESTIONS

Am I comfortable thinking of myself as powerful?

Who can I look to for support as I work to wield my power wisely and justly?

What is my go-to conflict management style?

What style am I least comfortable with?

Do I have effective techniques for dealing with my own anger?

When and with whom do I find myself being seen through one of the paradigms—as daughter, mother, or wife? Can I disrupt that pattern?

3

Finding Joy in Your Work

———

THE JOYS OF LEADERSHIP are many. Almost every day brings a deeply pleasurable event or two. Most of my time is spent with interesting and engaging people who are, like me, deeply committed to our institution's mission. I regularly see the positive impact of decisions I have made. I am able to support the efforts of our dedicated faculty and staff and see the ways that they in turn make a difference in the lives of our students. I know that my work matters. It matters to our students, and it matters to the world they will enter.

Finding joy in your work is essential for your own happiness. But it is also a requisite part of doing the work well. Nothing substitutes for your own enthusiasm and passion. A positive perspective keeps you committed and inspires everyone with whom you work. It is not selfish to want to enjoy yourself in your job. And it isn't a virtue to keep hanging on to work that makes you miserable.

Some years ago, I hosted a gathering of provosts at my house for dinner. They were on our campus for meetings that focused on various collaborative projects. As we finished eating, I asked each of them to stand and share a success story with us—something that happened on their campus in the past year that made them proud. The stories were amazing. Some of them focused on big, public achievements: a new building dedicated or a new academic program developed. But most—in the context of this supportive group of understanding colleagues—shared quieter, private victories. We heard about the resolution to a long-standing departmental feud, a failing student who was coached to graduation, and the gentle support provided to a colleague facing a life-threatening medical diagnosis. These victories don't appear in any annual report. Many are known only to those involved. But it is here that so much of the deep satisfaction of leadership can be found.

In addition to the pleasure of performing engaging, meaningful work, leadership offers the satisfaction that comes with meeting a challenge and living with integrity. Leadership is extremely hard work and often meets resistance and roadblocks. No matter how well you do your job, there are those who will believe it should have been done better. Critics are vocal, letting you know when they don't like a decision or when you are not paying enough attention to something they think is important. Moreover, many of the problems you are asked to solve are long standing and deeply rooted. Competing interests make it hard to find common ground. The tradition of shared governance means that even the wisest solutions have to be vetted and reviewed.

As a woman, you are often held to a higher standard. You are asked to prove yourself again and again. In addition to engaging in this difficult work and doing it well, you are pressured to exhibit the traits associated with feminine success, such as warmth, availability, and attractiveness.

No wonder that some women conclude the work is too unpleasant or too hard to be worth doing.

When women ask how they can experience more happiness in their work, I often invite them to read Marcus Aurelius's *Meditations*. Written during his reign as emperor of Rome and influenced by the Stoic thinking of his day, *Meditations* is a guidebook for finding lasting happiness as a leader. According to Aurelius, the wise leader doesn't look to fleeting popularity or fame. The adulation of crowds comes and goes. The only way to find joy as a leader, he says, is to build your happiness on the one thing that is in your control: the integrity of your actions. For him, this means that happiness has be grounded in the internal satisfaction that comes from having done what is right and good: "If you do the job in a principled way, with diligence, energy, and patience, if you keep yourself free of distractions, and keep the spirit inside you undamaged, as if you might have to give it back at any moment. . . . If you can embrace this without fear or expectations—can find fulfillment in what you are doing now, as Nature intended, and in superhuman truthfulness (every word, every utterance)—then your life will be happy. No one can prevent that."[1]

Aurelius reminds us that we might be tempted to bend to the loudest voices or to curry favor with an influential faction. We might think that the pleasure that comes from popularity is what we are after. But that kind of pleasure—even if we enjoy it—is fleeting. There is no way to make everyone happy for very long. Realizing this is a kind of freedom. It frees us to do the right thing and to draw our pleasure from the more lasting satisfaction of acting with integrity. On the days when critical emails fill your in-box or you have a meeting with a grouchy complainer, Aurelius offers comfort and support.

It is worth noting the importance Aurelius gives to truth telling as part of happiness. I talk about the importance of transparency and about the difference between secrecy and privacy in chapter 4, but the connection to happiness is well worth noting.

When you tell the truth, you do not have to carry the weight of keeping a secret. You remove the possibility that you can be pressured into doing something wrong in order to prevent someone from telling your secret. Moreover, by not keeping unpleasant news a secret, you share the burden of the truth with others, who also have to absorb and respond to it. Secret keeping is a psychological burden. And in this day and age, the truth is likely to come to light at some point anyway. You can save yourself a lot of psychic pain by committing to telling the truth and leading in a transparent way.

True happiness in your work may involve more than the Stoic satisfaction in doing your work with integrity. So it is worth reviewing the things that you find deeply pleasurable about your work. I recommend making a written list and updating it regularly. Mine looks like this:

- leading meaningful change
- inspiring my institution to live up to its highest values
- being part of a first-rate team
- opportunities to speak, write, and create
- being part of a dynamic intellectual community
- representing the college and its values locally, nationally, and internationally
- learning something new almost every day
- meeting with interesting people almost every day
- inspiring others to lead and serve
- serving as a role model for women and other people who have been underrepresented in leadership roles

This is a very personal list. The parts of your work that give you joy are likely to be different than mine. As you make your own list, ask yourself, what makes me think "job well done"? Where do I find meaning in my work? What do I look forward to? What do I bring to my job that others could not?

Keeping this list close by where you can review it regularly—especially on difficult days—will help you remember the positive aspects of your job. You can also see what changes over time. The list is for your eyes alone, so don't be afraid to write down the things that truly make you happy—even if they seem silly or like a guilty pleasure. If sitting at the head table or crowning the homecoming queen brings you joy, it belongs on your list.

Overcoming Barriers to Happiness

The visibility of leadership means that you have to contend with personal criticism. Different from critical responses to a decision or plan you have made, personal criticism has you as a target. It might be a snide remark about your style or personality. It might be someone letting you know that "other people" don't like you. It might be an overheard imitation of the way you talk or behave. It might be an angry parent who veers from an institutional complaint to a more personal attack.

When this kind of negativity comes from other women, it can be particularly painful. It calls up memories of the mean girls at the lunch table. It is a reminder of the dark side of female competitiveness—the sense that one woman's success is threatening to everyone else. And women often know exactly where another woman's vulnerability lies.

My husband calls these mean little encounters "spider bites." He reminds me that even when I know the spider isn't deadly, it still hurts to be bitten, and I still have to metabolize the venom. Acknowledging the wound, taking some time to let the hurt course through me and subside, and then giving myself permission to let it go is helpful. We can't prevent spider bites, but we can keep from renewing the poison.

This metaphor is also a reminder to quash any spider tendency of your own. Not only is it an unpleasant character trait, but it can have negative consequences for your career. People see and remember who shares nasty gossip and who speaks negatively. The world of higher education is small, and you never know if the person you disrespected will later be in a position to provide an opportunity or a reference.

The ubiquity of social media means that one angry spider can spew venom widely and even anonymously. This kind of criticism is difficult to respond to because of its amorphous and ever-changing nature. It is best to not engage and to save your communication for more direct venues. In the midst of a Twitter attack or a coordinated email campaign, it can be tempting to try to defend yourself at every turn. But communication experts recommend letting the wave of negative communication wash over you and then responding in a general and public manner. Sharing as much of the truth as privacy regulations allow, sticking to the principles of your institution and your own values, and deputizing others to share key messages are all helpful strategies. You cannot control what other people say, but you can continue to live and lead with integrity.

Stress is another barrier to overcome. No one is surprised that leadership is demanding. Concern about managing stress is a key reason women cite when they tell me they are reluctant to aspire to senior positions.

Paradoxically, I find I handle my stress better when I don't let myself think or talk about it as a general state. "Stress" is almost always a cover story—a way of not noticing or not saying what I am actually feeling. There isn't anything inherently wrong with using this shorthand, but when I don't take the time to get crystal clear about what lies behind my stress, it looms larger and sticks around longer.

The next time you are feeling stress, I invite you to pause and try to get a more specific handle on your experience. Usually I find that "I had a stressful day" means "there were times during the day when I experienced negative feelings." The vagueness of the term "stress" covers over the details of those bad feelings and allows me to sweep them all together without thinking too much about any of them.

What happens when you unpack your stress? If you are like me, you will find a bunch of unpleasant feelings. Depending on the day, that emotion might be anger, sadness, frustration, fear, shame, embarrassment, or anxiety.

Why was the meeting stressful? Because I was furious with my colleague and also embarrassed that I wasn't better prepared. Why am I feeling stressed as I head home today? Because my report is going to be late, and I am afraid I will be fired. Getting to the root feeling means that I can look for a solution. Sometimes, just saying it out loud helps me feel more in control. Sometimes, I have to plan a response. Sometimes, I have to remind myself that one late report isn't the end of my job.

As long as I am focused on the undifferentiated mass of stress, those coping tools can't come into play. So why do we stay at the level of the general?

Often, it is because we don't want to face the more specific emotions. Many women have learned to avoid expressing anger—and even to avoid recognizing when we are feeling anger. But when I ask women to describe their stress in more concrete terms, I often hear stories about anger. The anger is usually directed toward a particular person—a difficult colleague, a demanding boss, a student or alum with unreasonable demands—and often the woman isn't fully aware of the strength of her own anger until she says it out loud as she sorts out the causes of her stress.

Fear is another common cause of stress. Think about the last time you felt threatened by something that happened at work. You might have been afraid of losing your job, of damage to your reputation or the reputation of the college, or of some other kind of harm. It is likely that your fear was on the edge of your consciousness—you knew that you were feeling bad but might not have reflected on the content of the bad feeling. As a result, your fear gets lumped under the broader category of stress.

The best antidote to anger and fear is to name them. Getting clearer about exactly what you are feeling makes the emotions much more manageable. When I look at my fears head on, I usually find that they are pretty tame. When they are held within the great big blob known as stress, they keep me up at night. But when I say them directly and out loud, they usually sound pretty ridiculous. After all, it is unlikely that the events of any given day are going to result in an actual disaster for me or my institution.

Fear can be a tricky emotion for leaders. A certain amount of catastrophizing—thinking about the worst possible outcome of any decision or event—is necessary for effective leadership. A good leader has to remain vigilant against external threats and has to think about the potential negative consequences of her actions. Remaining attentive to your worst fears helps you do your job. But a focus on negative outcomes can easily become overwhelming.

Finding the balance between appropriate defensive thinking and anxiety-based worrying is an ongoing practice. I try to limit myself to scenarios both that are likely and that have possible preventive solutions. When wilder disasters cross my mind, I aim to limit their ability to disrupt my thinking.

Shame is another emotional trap for women. We have often internalized the message that we aren't good enough. It doesn't take much to push most of us into reciting the story of our inadequacies. Impostor syndrome is ubiquitous. Noticing how much of our stress is really about shame is an important step in releasing the hold shame has on us. Brené Brown's writing is a helpful place to start if you find that shame is undermining your happiness at work.[2]

Energy Management for Happiness

Exhaustion is a key component of stress. As leaders, our days are likely to be jam-packed. Managing our time, however, isn't enough to prevent burnout. We also have to manage our physical, psychic, and spiritual energy.

I have developed specific practices to help me in this. To start, I explicitly distinguish between the aspects of my work that I find energizing and the aspects that deplete me. The energizing side of my list includes spending time with creative people, making meaningful decisions, writing, learning something new, and eating a healthy lunch. The depleting side includes listening to complaints, attending events that start after 8:00 p.m., and sitting still for long periods. I aim to be very specific and completely honest as I make this list. It is for my eyes alone, so I don't have to worry about what it says about me or whether it will hurt someone's feelings to find out they are on my depleting list.

The list serves as a guide as I plan my schedule. I try not to have too many depleting things in one week or go too long in any day without scheduling something that fills me with energy. Knowing what depletes me means I can give myself a psychic pat on the back when I manage to get through them. Knowing what energizes me helps me anticipate and appreciate them even more.

Some depleting activities can be limited or delegated. But there are many that can't or shouldn't. I find that just acknowledging that I am about to do something unpleasant or hard takes the edge off, and I am sometimes surprised that it turns out to be less onerous than expected. And even if it is hard, I can jump right in to something I enjoy.

You may want to take this energy analysis even deeper. In reflecting on my own energy and moods, I find that I tend to flow among five basic energetic states: radiating, absorbing, ruminating, deflecting, and integrating.

Radiating is the term I use for activities in which my energy is moving from inside to outside. I am open and sharing something of myself. For me, these activities include hosting events, strategizing, public speaking, and writing. These radiating activities bring me a lot of joy, but they have a negative potential to deplete me if I overdo it.

Absorbing activities are those where energy is moving from outside me to inside. I am receptive and listening. These include reading, listening to reports, and cultivating the talents of others. The positive aspect of these absorbing activities is the opportunity to gain new insights and to build bonds of understanding. But I can also become frustrated, angry, or sad if I have to absorb bad news or complaints.

I am prone to *ruminating* when my energy flows in an internal circle. This can have a positive side when it helps me solve problems. But it can also lead to anxiety if I don't interrupt the cycle of thought with action.

Deflecting occurs when I keep my energy focused outward without letting anything in. This is likely to appear as meaningless web surfing or disengagement from whatever is happening around me. This energetic state has a positive side in that it can offer rest and protection. Its negative aspect is that it can reinforce a sense of boredom or disengagement.

I love when I am able to engage in *integrating* activities, which I define as the merging of internal and external energies. Yoga, meditation, spending time with my husband and kids, walking in cities, having deep conversations with colleagues, visits with donors, visiting art museums, and discussing philosophy are all ways that I tap into integrating energy. These activities are inspiring and blissful. There isn't a negative side to integrating energy—except that it is impossible to maintain all the time.

If this strikes you as a useful framework, you can think of your own examples for each category. Be as honest as you can. Talking it over with someone who loves you might help you see things you might not even be aware of on your own.

The goal of understanding yourself in this way is not to eradicate everything unpleasant. That isn't possible. But you can aim to limit the negative effects of spending too much time in any one energy pattern, and you can maximize the pleasures inherent in each of them.

Work-Life Alignment

Happiness at work is impossible if you are aren't confident that you are meeting your responsibilities at home. As women leaders, we continue to have more responsibility for childcare and elder care than our male counterparts do.

Some years ago, I was the only woman on a senior leadership team, and we were working on a difficult project. It became clear we wouldn't finish by 5:30, and so the president suggested we order some pizzas and keep at it. We each picked up our phones to call home. As I was in the midst of explaining to my helpful and supportive husband how to finish the dinner I had started that morning—what to take out of the fridge, what had to be added, the timing and temperature, the side dish that needed to be completed—and reminding him that our daughter would need help with her math homework and our son had to finish a book report, I saw my male colleagues staring at me with surprise. After I hung up, one of them said, "All we had to do was call our wives to tell them we wouldn't be home for dinner." "But you *are* the wife," said another. These men were great colleagues, good husbands, and overall nice guys. I was fond of them. But until this moment, it hadn't occurred to them that in addition to our shared work, I had many more daily responsibilities at home than they did.

Even for women who are not mothers or whose children are grown, family responsibilities are likely to be pressing. Many of the women in my seminars are caring for elderly parents or siblings with disabilities. They have duties as daughters, sisters, and wives that are not easily shirked. Given the intensity and time commitment of senior leadership, it isn't surprising that one of the most common questions I am asked is about how to achieve work-life balance.

For a long time, I aimed for balance and never felt that I achieved it. I wound up feeling guilty no matter what I was doing. At work, I worried about the time I was not spending with my husband and children. At home, I worried about what I was not doing at work. When I took some time for myself, I felt I was failing at both of my roles. While I knew intellectually that the pressure to be both the perfect leader and the perfect wife and mother is an unrealistic expectation and a symptom of the inherent contradictions of womanhood under patriarchy, somehow this knowledge didn't result in an actual reduction in passing negative judgments on myself.

I found more overall satisfaction when I reoriented my thinking. I jettisoned the concept of balance in favor of the more useful idea of alignment. "Alignment" means reducing the friction between your work and the rest of your life so that the two fit more smoothly together. The less resistance there is between your job and everything else, the easier it is to meet your multiple responsibilities. Looking for ways to align my work and my life helps me be more effective at work and at home.

My husband and I use the concept of alignment in our big family decisions. For example, we have always chosen to live within walking distance of my office. This has meant we have needed to make compromises—sometimes our houses have been less fancy than we could afford, and sometimes they have been smaller or larger than would be optimal. We have narrowed our choices about schooling for our kids because our home neighborhood is tied to the college neighborhood. But these compromises have been worth it. Living near work means that I spend almost no time commuting. It means that my kids can stop by my office after school and that I can run home to check on a sick child or have lunch with my husband. For a long time, we only needed one car. Having the location of our house aligned with the location of my office eases stress and makes it easier to do what I need to in both places.

We also try to align our work travel as much as we can. When our kids were little, this meant we tried hard to travel on opposite schedules so one of us was always home. Now that they are grown, it means we aim to travel on the same schedule so we are home at the same time. My husband and I also plan our vacations around our work travel—meeting up when and where we can for a few days of play, accompanying each other when possible, and often choosing vacation spots based on where we can get in a bit of work. We compromise on where and when we go in order to make sure that we have as much time together as possible while still meeting our work obligations.

I choose my doctors and hairdresser based on their proximity to my work so I can run out in the middle of the day and not have to spend time driving back and forth. I shop online as much as I can and automate as many purchases as possible. When I became a president, I opted not to negotiate for club memberships and instead made sure the college provided me with sufficient household help so that I could actually do the job. Male presidents often don't need as much of this since they are more likely to have a wife who takes care of the household—sometimes as a paid member of the college staff. Women presidents are more likely to have a partner with a full-time job, and so we have to advocate for assistance in order to be able to spend as much time at work as our male peers. For me, extra household help was more valuable than other perks.

These examples are meant to be illustrative. You might find the compromises I have made are unworkable for you. But I hope they inspire you to think about how you can align your work and your life to maximize your happiness at both work and home. You will never achieve balance. Your work is going to take up lots of time, and you will have less time than you want to spend with your family and to take care of yourself. By aligning your work with the other things you care about, you can make the limited time you have more efficient and effective.

Finding joy in your work requires making the most of the pleasurable parts and minimizing the impact of the negative parts on your life and your well-being.

Putting It into Practice

In the midst of the day-to-day pressures of work, focusing on your own joy may seem selfish or secondary. But it is actually essential for good leadership. If your work doesn't bring you joy, you won't bring the best of yourself to it. Your creativity and passion will be siphoned off into other aspects of your life—or worse, go completely underground. This is a path toward unhappiness and burnout.

It is also a path toward disaster for your institution. Institutions flounder when leaders are hostile, afraid, or indifferent to the day-to-day efforts required to fulfill their missions. The mood of the leader seeps into the life of the institution. Only by finding and tending to your internal joy can you be a source of radiant joy for others.

REFLECTION QUESTIONS

What do I make of Aurelius's view that satisfaction comes from acting with integrity and not from external accolades?

Are there any secrets I can release?

What is on my happiness-at-work list? Can I do more of those activities?

Have I recently received a spider bite? How did I manage it?

When am I likely to feel stressed?

What are the underlying feelings that I subsume under the name "stress"?

Which work activities energize me? Which ones deplete me?

In which energy pattern (radiating, absorbing, ruminating, deflecting, integrating) am I spending most of my time?

Does my pattern need adjustment?

Are there ways to better align my life and my work?

4

Growing as a Leader

———

THE WOMEN in my seminars care deeply about leading well. They yearn to make a difference for their students and their institutions. But they also recognize that much of the day-to-day work feels narrowly focused. They see that they are spending much of their time reacting to problems and resolving them one at a time. They want to get better at setting an agenda for change that could move their institutions forward in a more holistic way. They don't want to simply manage, they want to lead. They wonder what leadership means and how to do it effectively.

Because leadership is complex and often misunderstood, it can be hard to know if we are doing a good job—hard even to know the standards by which leadership should be judged. Do we measure success in terms of the happiness of our faculty and staff? the achievements of our students? the engagement of our alumni? the size of the annual fund? presidential longevity? institutional rate of change? A case could be made for any or all of these—but it is almost impossible to maximize them all at once. Sometimes, we have to accept a short-term setback in one area in pursuit of a larger goal.

Aristotle argued that without a clear target, it is impossible to improve your aim.[1] In this chapter, I invite you to home in on the bull's-eye of success by developing a richer understanding of the meaning of effective leadership in an academic context.

Growing as a leader requires practice and reflection. Many women find that leadership is not merely a set of skills or a list of tasks. It is a deeply personal, indeed a spiritual, discipline. As a leader, my values—not the ones I might give lip service to but the ones I am actually willing to go to the mat for—are constantly on display. Opportunities for self-deception are few since my actions are broadly visible and open to public evaluation. Having to make daily decisions about the best way to use limited resources, about which of the infinite problems deserve part of my finite attention, and about how to navigate criticism and not be swayed by praise is a near-constant lesson in character building. These hard choices force me to reckon with my limitations and motivate me to make the very best use of my strengths. Like the biblical Jacob, I wrestle nightly with angels and almost always walk away with both a blessing and a limp. It is the hardest work I have ever done. And the most meaningful.

Embracing the spiritual aspects of leadership—using whatever metaphors are most meaningful to you—may help you muster the inner strength to face the challenges. My hardest moments at work are when I let my leadership style wander too far from my essential core self. In the moments when I forget to let my values shine through, forget to listen and learn, or forget to take a break to replenish, I am most likely to make a poor decision or to act in ways that undermine my goals. Sometimes, this takes the form of snapping at a colleague or getting behind in responding to email. Other times, it means losing focus on the most important ways to use my time and energy.

Women have fewer cultural models of leadership to draw on and fewer opportunities for a same-sex mentor or sponsor. We have to create—rather than merely emulate—a paradigm for women's leadership. This additional burden is draining, but it is also freeing. When

I am told, "You don't look like a college president," I channel Gloria Steinem and say, "This is what a college president looks like." In other words, the way we do it is the way it is done.

There are some reasons to think that women lead differently—and often better—than men. A report in the *Harvard Business Review* cites research that found that women are rated higher by their peers on 84 percent of leadership skills.[2] According to the study's authors, Jack Zenger and Joseph Folkman, women excel in skills such as "taking initiative, acting with resilience, practicing self-development, driving for results, and displaying high integrity and honesty." The only areas where men were consistently rated higher than women were "develops strategic perspective" and "technical or professional expertise." Men were also found to have greater confidence than women, especially early in their careers. The authors hypothesize that young men's unearned confidence may actually hinder their development of leadership skills. Since they don't believe they need to develop additional skills, they don't engage in the learning activities that would help them improve.

The *Chronicle of Higher Education* reports that as of 2019, 30 percent of college presidents are women. That number is bolstered by the number of female community college presidents since women comprise 36 percent of that sector. Over fifteen years, the percentage of women leading all types of institutions has risen from 21 percent. In asking if women lead differently, Lee Gardner identifies areas where women have an edge.[3] She argues that women are more likely to lead in a collaborative and communal manner. We are more likely to build community and less likely to run our institutions in ways that are arrogant or self-centered.

While it is tempting to pat ourselves on the back or claim superiority, we need to treat these kinds of claims with a healthy skepticism. Our leadership styles have likely been shaped by our experience. Because women have to navigate deeply rooted biases, we learn to adjust our leadership style to avoid or reduce resistance. Because we encounter heightened expectations about our empathy and ability to create a supportive environment, we learn to create a collaborative culture. Male arrogance and a top-down management style are often seen as signs of strength and executive presence. A woman rarely has the option of leading that way since those same traits will count against her in the hiring and evaluation process. Gardner points out that women are more likely to be "punished" for using a dominant leadership style and more likely to be expected to be accessible and inclusive. In other words, as in so many other things, you may have to be better than your male peers in order to be given the same opportunities.

Leadership in the Academy

Amazon carries 60,000 books about leadership—almost all of which are focused on leading for-profit businesses and thus make numerous assumptions that don't translate well into higher education. The business-oriented books assume that profit is the ultimate aim and that the CEO has a great deal of unilateral control. And because businesses are almost exclusively focused on short-term profit, rarely do these books consider the leader's responsibility to the past or to the distant future. They may give lip service to some higher mission, but ultimately their goal is to help the reader lead in such a way as to make a lot of money in a short period of time.

There are three primary reasons that the model of business leadership often doesn't apply to a higher education context. The first is that in higher education, we start with the mission rather than with profit as our goal. Our institutions exist to provide an education for our students. Our business model serves that mission rather than the other way around. We are not interested in profit—in fact, we reinvest any surplus back into the mission—and our time horizon is infinitely long. Every decision we make has to improve the institution not only for the people present in this moment, but for the generations to come. Our assets have been given to us in trust—either directly by our students for their education or indirectly on their behalf through endowments, government grants, or gifts to the annual fund. We are responsible as well to those who have come before us, who built and nurtured our institutions for a hundred years or more.

A second difference is that governance in higher education is more complex than in the typical business. Our employees, particularly those with tenure, see themselves as partners in the enterprise. They expect to have a say in what happens. Many intend to serve their entire career at our institution. They know that they will outlast deans and presidents and board chairs. They have seen strategic plans come and go. They are prepared to wait out bad ideas and ineffective leadership. They are not easily fooled nor are they attracted to the latest management fad. Explicit and implicit governance norms are in place to protect our mission, making radical change difficult.

Finally, while our students often bring a consumerist mindset with them, fundamentally they are not our customers. Our job is not to please them but to educate them. A true education is hard, and the process is often uncomfortable. Unlike customers, students have to meet certain standards in order to "purchase" our "product," and neither they nor we expect that they are always right or will always be happy.

Leading a college clearly isn't the same as leading a business, but this doesn't mean that there isn't great value in the business-oriented leadership books. Understanding basic management skills, financial planning, and marketing paradigms is essential for effective leadership no matter the context. I learn a lot from reading business books, talking with experienced business leaders, and exploring the trends described in the *Harvard Business Review*. Like most of my presidential peers, my formal education did not include training in business, and I have had to learn those skills on the job. But there is more to effectively leading a college or university than what is in those books.

If academic leadership isn't the same as leading a for-profit business, is there something else that serves as a better analogy? You sometimes hear that being a college president is a bit like being the mayor of a small town. That is a helpful image because it addresses both the complexity and the intimacy of a college or university. And it reminds us of the ways that academic leaders are expected to serve their campuses.

In his book *Positive Academic Leadership*, Jeffrey L. Buller notes that academic leaders can be variously compared to coaches, counselors, and conductors.[4] Sometimes, presidents or deans are compared to a family patriarch. Sexism aside, that analogy too has some validity in that the president is expected to be concerned both about the institution's legacy and about the well-being of all of its members. But like all analogies, the similarities are matched by equally pertinent differences.

Defining Leadership

Because there is no exact comparison, I have spent time thinking carefully about the work we do as leaders in higher education. This chapter reflects my current understanding of my own work and what I have learned over time through experience, reading, and conversations with others. Certainly, other presidents have different insights and ways of conceptualizing what they do and how they lead, and I encourage you to seek multiple perspectives and ideas.

Developing as a leader is a lot like developing as a writer or teacher. It is a matter of finding your own voice rather than copying a model or unthinkingly following a set of "rules." Also like writing and teaching, different voices are called for in different situations. A repertoire of expressive possibilities and a deep sense of what drives the work create a more likely path to success than a whole bunch of how-to books or leadership theories. In my seminars, I encourage women to think about their own leadership styles. We discuss leaders we admire, the times when we feel we have led in productive ways, and the times we have failed. From these experiences, we draw tentative conclusions about what is effective, and then we test them in real situations.

Over time, I have developed a working definition of leadership that frames our conversations:

Leadership is the practice of ideas and actions that inspire others to make positive change.

The words in that definition are important to me—"practice," "inspire others," "positive," "change."

I think of leadership as a practice in the same way I think of time on my yoga mat as a practice or my writing as a practice. They all require personal development, the abilities to self-reflect and to accept critique, and the tenaciousness to keep getting better over time. When I took my first presidency, I imagined that my job was to solve every problem and get the institution to an "end point" of perfection. I soon learned that this was a faulty model. Like yoga, writing, and raising children, the resolution of one challenge is exciting and satisfying—and immediately leads to another challenge. There is no moment of "finishing" or "being done." There are only moments of steering through this week's rapids and learning how to avoid repeating the same problems over and over. There are also signs of success, comparable to the publication of an article, mastering a new yoga pose, or teaching a child to tie their shoes. Celebrate your sense of happiness and pride in your new abilities and the opportunities for your institution. And then go right back to work to move to the next level.

I have come to see that inspiring change is the essence of effective leadership, and I contrast that with the effective management that is needed in times and areas of stasis. In our roles as deans, provosts, vice presidents, and presidents, we are called on to do both of these things.

Good management is essential to oversee projects and processes and to measure compliance and effectiveness. Management work is demanding and requires skill and energy to do well. I work with many outstanding managers, and my own portfolio includes many areas where management is the most important thing I can offer. Good management keeps things working as they are set up to do.

But it is leadership that creates change. It resets the dial and creates new structures, new solutions, and new ways of doing things—all of which then require management. Leadership is what allows the limits of the current system to be recognized, and then it builds a better alternative. In an era where change is preeminent and where even the strongest institutions are remaking themselves to respond to economic and demographic pressures, strong leadership is essential for higher education.

Leadership is hard in part because it is inherently relational. A strong personality with a lot of structural power can demand change and issue orders. But those changes are unlikely to outlast that individual's time in office. Only by inspiring others to believe in and enact new ways of doing things can a leader make a fundamental change in an institution.

A great example of this is the work that my predecessor at Rhodes, Bill Troutt, did to reorient the relationship Rhodes has with its home city of Memphis. Bill saw that the college needed to claim its urban identity and integrate its educational mission with service to the city. Rhodes needed to develop a unique brand as well as further its mission to "graduate students with a lifelong passion for learning, a compassion for others, and the ability to translate academic study and personal concern into effective leadership and action in their communities and the world." Working closely with campus leaders, especially Vice President Russ Wigginton and Provost Milton Moreland, President Troutt inspired faculty members, staff, and students to embrace the city. Faculty began offering service-learning courses, and new partnerships were forged with nonprofit organizations and for-profit companies. Decisions at the college were made with the city and its needs and opportunities in mind. Because this new vision inspired so many, its effect persisted after the original leaders moved on. "Liberal arts in the city" has taken on a life of its own at Rhodes and is deep in the bloodstream of our campus and the students we attract.

During her presidency, Elizabeth Kiss led Agnes Scott College to reframe its mission around a new core curriculum as a way of refreshing the value of a women's college. Using a deeply dialogic and interactive process, the campus met Kiss's challenge to address the changing needs of its women students. The result is a model of learning called Summit, which, according to the college's website, "reinvents a liberal arts education for the 21st century by preparing every student to be an effective change agent in a global society. Guided by a personal board of advisors, every student, regardless of major, designs an individualized course of study and co-curricular experiences that develop leadership abilities and understanding of complex global dynamics."

What these examples share is the inspirational and collective nature of the changes. Institutional transformation is never the work of a single person. It requires decentralized, ongoing change and decision-making across time and space. Good leaders envision and inspire, but they never make change alone.

Understanding leadership as an active practice and not as a professional title or job has helped me see the way that leadership emerges at multiple levels. We all know people with fancy titles who fail to lead. We also know that some of the world's best and most important leaders have inspired others without holding an office, a title, or a formal perch. This is particularly true on a college campus where multiple constituents have opportunities to inspire change.

Figuring Out What Needs to Change

If leadership means inspiring change, then defining what needs to change is one of the key powers and responsibilities of leaders. One college president said that the main work of the presidency is deciding what you are going to pay attention to. Your focus is your most important and effective tool. Another said that "choosing your battles" is essential for success.

Sometimes, the focus of your attention is identified as part of the hiring process. You may be told things such as "we need to increase enrollment" or "improve standards" or "globalize our curriculum." As soon as you land in your new job, you are inundated with other recommendations for change—in the form of complaints and proposals—from many corners of the campus. During the liminal period I described in chapter 1, you will likely also identify potential problems that might not yet be seen as issues by those who are living in their midst.

Your first step is to sort through this information and determine what has priority and how you will speak about and learn more about those top concerns. It may seem overwhelming. How do you decide where to focus? How do you begin to imagine the future?

In my leadership work, I have developed a three-cornered framework for identifying the kind of changes needed and the leadership work I must do. At the most general level, I think in terms of three institutional aspects: mission, business model, and culture. An institution is healthy only when these are in alignment.

The genius of US higher education is the multiplicity of institutional missions. There are universities focused on the creation of new knowledge, liberal arts colleges devoted solely to undergraduate intellectual development, technical colleges, institutions that were founded to serve special populations, community colleges, and on and on. None of these missions is better or worse than any other. Each offers unique options for students and has an important role to play in the overall landscape of higher education in the United States.

But whatever its mission, the institution has to have an underlying business model—a structure for generating revenues and allocating funds for expenses—that supports that mission. A good business decision for one kind of mission could be disastrous for another. For example, a large research university might wisely use graduate teaching assistants to supplement instruction in a large lecture course. This saves money and also allows the institution to live out its mission by training the next generation of faculty. For a small liberal arts college, however, the financial savings generated by hiring graduate students to teach would be outweighed by the loss of tuition revenue from students who only choose that institution because of the access to full-time faculty.

Finally, the institutional culture can support or undermine the mission and business model. Culture includes everything from how students address their professors to what institutional milestones are marked with what kind of ceremony. As an institution attempts to change, aspects of its culture might be a drag on change. Other aspects might be harnessed to drive change.

To me, a leader's job is to align these three pillars under a single unifying vision. I have spent my career at three colleges that have many similarities. They are all intimate, high-quality liberal arts colleges, all founded in 1848 or 1849, and all dedicated to educating talented traditionally aged college students. But each lived out the mission-culture-business model in a different way. Each needed focus on a different aspect of this triangle.

When I arrived at Austin College, it was in the midst of transforming its mission to focus on serving a more diverse student body and creating opportunities for students to access a high-quality liberal arts education no matter their financial background. The campus culture already had pivoted in this direction and was supportive, inclusive, and student-focused. But the new mission hadn't been clearly articulated, and the financial model wasn't connecting revenues and expenses in ways that could support the new direction.

Muhlenberg College had a stable financial model and a culture that encouraged individual effort, but at the time I became provost, it needed to develop a stronger sense of its mission and deepen the cultural engagement with that mission.

At Rhodes College, we are building on a strong sense of mission as we focus on creating a culture that supports belonging and inclusive thriving. We are also making sure that our business model continues to evolve in response to changing external market conditions.

In each case, we used a current strength as a foundation of the triangle and then worked on bringing the other two points into alignment with that cornerstone. It gave us a shared place to stand and a sense of confidence even as we made change.

One of the most important things we do as leaders is to identify and reflect back the unique trifecta of mission, business model, and culture that makes up our particular institution. Finding resonant language to articulate the ways they align or misalign and tying strategic initiatives to creating alignment are important uses of rhetorical leadership.

There was a time when culture, mission, and business model could be viewed as separate tracks. The faculty understood themselves as the guardians of the mission and didn't feel the need to concern themselves with how the college functioned as a business or what the student experience and culture were like. The board focused on the business model and left the mission and culture to the academic affairs and student life departments, respectively. And the student life professionals kept their focus solely on the students.

Contemporary higher education is so complex that this kind of siloed thinking is not only outdated, it is threatening to the health of our industry. Good boards now know that any real progress on strengthening the business model has implications for the college's mission. They understand as well that the campus culture drives everything from how students learn to what they are willing to pay. Similarly, engaged faculty and staff understand that the business model can't be divorced from the educational mission.

If your institution or program is facing problems, you need a diagnosis. Perhaps the business model no longer supports the mission. Perhaps the campus culture is at odds with the ways you raise revenue. You have to decide what needs to change in order to achieve alignment. In some cases, a new business model can be imagined. In others, the mission will have to be adjusted to reflect market realities and opportunities. In some cases, efforts will need to be made to remake the campus culture so that it supports the kinds of students who are enrolling. Creating a vision of a successful future is the subject of the next chapter.

Positive Change

Once you have identified that change is needed, it is your job to lead it. In his book *Leading Change*, noted author and consultant John P. Kotter identifies the eight stages of creating significant change:

1. Establish a sense of urgency.
2. Create the guiding coalition.
3. Develop a vision and strategy.
4. Communicate the change vision.
5. Empower broad-based action.

6. Generate short-term wins.
7. Consolidate gains and produce more wins.
8. Anchor new approaches to the culture.[5]

This method is useful whether you are contemplating a major change (e.g., redesigning the core curriculum or establishing branch campuses) or more minor ones (e.g., revising the publication standards in your department or creating a new orientation program).

Sometimes, the urgency is obvious: a budget or enrollment crisis emerges and demands immediate action. This can make the work of establishing the need to change both easier and harder. It is easier because it is clear the status quo is not working. It is harder because panic and crisis are not conducive to reasoned debate and assessment. Often, finger-pointing and over-the-top rhetoric arise. Instead of accepting the changing market conditions, the prevailing analyses become polarized and focused on singular scapegoats: "the dean is undermining the liberal arts," "the president hates the faculty," "the faculty members refuse to change," "the students are terrible." As a leader, it is important to resist these simplistic explanations and help your community understand the complex factors that have given rise to the current crisis. The earlier you can do this and the more detailed information you can provide, the more likely it is that your narrative will prevail.

It can be more difficult to lead when there is no obvious crisis because it is harder for others to see why change is necessary. As the leader, you can see trouble on the horizon—a mounting need for financial aid, demographic changes, an unstable economic climate—but as long as it isn't causing an immediate and visible problem, it is easy for others to minimize or ignore it.

Part of your job as a leader is to manage urgency. In times of active crisis, you have to buoy hope and inspire people to work together. In times of steady decline—when the actual crisis is still in the future—you have to help your community understand the looming threat without creating panic. As a leader in higher education, your words are the most powerful tool at your disposal. The way you describe the institution's situation, the language you use to articulate a vision, and the ways you speak about the potential future determine almost everything about what can be accomplished.

Sometimes, our language is out of date or not in keeping with our campus's culture. Speaking about diversity on a campus that has reoriented itself toward inclusion or social justice can strike others as out of touch. Ignoring new conventions around pronoun use, stumbling over unfamiliar names, and assuming others' familiarity with your own religious or cultural tradition will exclude many of the people you need to engage.

For women, who are expected to be more empathic than men, the cost of mistakes in language use can be higher. I encourage my colleagues to correct me if I misspeak, and I reach out to campus experts for advice about how to best communicate when discussing issues with which I am unfamiliar. I try to apologize when I make a mistake.

Because communication is so essential to your success, I recommend taking every public speaking opportunity seriously. Even the briefest and most informal set of remarks—welcoming new faculty, greeting visiting parents during a family weekend, making a few remarks at a reception—is a chance to articulate your vision and to tie the present event into a broader sense of the institution's meaning. I encourage you to write your own speeches, but if writing isn't a strength, hire a speechwriter who will take the time to really understand your vision and message and convey them in words that are true to you.

The Disruptor President

Change should never be made simply for its own sake. There is a certain type of president—often a man—that likes the position of "disruptor" or "change agent." They pride themselves on doing things differently than their predecessors—toward whom they are often condescending. They exude confidence and imply that they will save the institution through the force of their unique skills and their iconoclastic courage. They often use language imported from commerce or technology.

This kind of masculine swagger can be very attractive to boards. It matches what they may know in the business world and gives the illusion that the institution's problems have a quick fix. Male arrogance is easily confused with competence, and it is easy to understand why this kind of candidate can be successful in a presidential search. There are some women who can get away with this kind of persona, but it is more likely that a woman's arrogance will turn off board members instead.

These disruptor presidencies almost always end quickly and often do real damage to the institution. The problem is not that a change-maker can't succeed. Most successful presidents are strong leaders of change. The problem is that this character type is focused on his own identity as a maverick and not on the specific needs of the institution he has been asked to lead. Presidents like this make decisions based on their own imagined "brand," which may not be what is best for everyone else.

One such president eradicated key academic departments. Another announced (without a stable financial plan in place) that all students would be required to study abroad. A third immediately scrapped the college's beloved logo and colors and replaced them with a design by a consultant friend of his. There are moments when any of these could be good ideas—and there are examples of great presidents who have accomplished all three. But in these cases, the changes signaled something about the disruptor nature of the president and were not grounded in a deep, research-based understanding of the institution or its market.

Making Decisions

One of the things that surprised me when I became a provost and that has remained true during my time as a president is the sheer volume of decisions I am expected to make in a day. I learned quickly that the phenomenon of "decision fatigue" is very real.[6] This is a psychological term that measures the energy expenditures associated with decision-making. It describes fatigue concerning the *number* of decisions you make, not their intensity or difficulty. Wise leaders do everything they can to reduce the number of unimportant decisions they have to make in order to save their energy for the ones that really matter.

President Barack Obama talked about this explicitly when he explained that he had reduced his professional wardrobe to a series of dark suits. Tech leaders are famous for adopting daily uniforms. They literally wear the same thing every day, spending no time at all choosing an outfit. Men have a much easier time of this, of course, although women's magazines and podcasts tout the efficiency of a capsule wardrobe for women that limits your clothing choices to just a few items.

I have managed to create as simple a "uniform" as I can, given the pressures I am under to look professional and well-dressed. I usually choose a fitted shift dress in a neutral solid color, boots or shoes with a stylish but comfortable block or wedge heel, and black tights or sheer stockings. I wear a version of this almost every day. My other alternative is a black suit (with either a skirt or trousers) and a colored silk blouse. I have automated my clothes shopping by ordering online from a few vendors with reliable sizing.

But even if you automate your closet and other aspects of your life, such as meal planning, you are still asked to make multiple decisions every day. Delegate as many of them as you reasonably can. Then create a strategy for the rest.

By the time an issue gets to your desk for a decision, there are likely to be many people on standby who can't move forward until you provide direction. One of the most common complaints I hear about provosts and presidents is that they can't make a timely decision. This will irritate those who directly report to you no end. The longer it takes you, the more institutional energy is wasted.

You don't want to make hasty decisions, but you need to make them with all due speed. This means you have to get good at understanding what you need to know in order to decide. When I find that I am having trouble making a decision, it is usually because of one of the following reasons:

I don't have enough information.
I don't like any of the options that have been presented.
I know what has to be done, but I don't want to do it.

If lack of knowledge is the issue, aim to get very clear about what exactly you want to know before deciding. Ask if that information can be provided to you and how costly (in time and money) it will be to get it. Often, you can hold off on a decision until you have the right information. Sometimes, however, you have to take a risk and decide without having all the facts.

If you don't like the options, see if you or your team can come up with alternatives. Perhaps what has been offered depends on an assumption that can be waived or altered. Or maybe there is a synthesis or a third way. If this can be found, the decision becomes easier, but sometimes you have to grit your teeth and choose the lesser of two evils.

It is common to be in the third situation. In your heart, you know what has to be done. But you are hesitating because it will make someone unhappy or cause a hassle of some sort. This is a good time to read Marcus Aurelius and then go ahead and do what is right.

The clearer you are about your vision and about how you want to align the mission, the culture, and the business model, the easier it will be to determine the right path.

Transparency

One of the most valued skills in a leader is transparency—the willingness to share how decisions are made and the reasons behind them. In thinking about transparency, I find it helpful to distinguish between privacy and secrecy. Private matters are things we keep out of view because they are intimate. The general facts might be widely known, but the details are not for public consumption. Brushing your teeth and using the bathroom are examples of private matters. You might be embarrassed to be seen doing them, but you wouldn't be ashamed. Secrets, on the other hand, are inherently shameful. A secret is something that can't be known by others. It has to be kept in order to avoid some unpleasant consequence.

There are many things you know in your work that have to be kept private—usually for legal reasons but also to protect the privacy of others. Student privacy is covered under the Family Educational Rights and Privacy Act. Employee privacy may be mandated as part of a settlement agreement or may be an important institutional or personal value. Keeping private matters private is part of your job.

Keeping secrets, however, should be avoided at all costs. You might think you are not in danger of keeping institutional secrets because you would never do anything illegal or immoral. But secret keeping can creep up on you. Would you be ashamed to have your email read out loud? Have you withheld important information about the college's budget from the board or the faculty? Did you make a personnel decision that wasn't quite fair?

Secrets are dangerous for a variety of reasons. They give anyone who knows the secret power over you. They almost always come out in the end. And they are a sign of personal weakness. But for the purposes of this book, I want to emphasize that secrets are bad because they steal your joy. You have to invest energy in keeping them and worrying about them. When they do come out, you have to spend time in damage control. A secret makes it hard to rest.

Transparency is good in itself. It makes you a stronger and more respected leader. And it is good for what it brings: peace of mind and a clear conscience.

The Virtues of Good Leadership

As individuals, we each have a stake in doing our work well. We want to shine and succeed. But the impulse to aim for excellence takes on a new urgency when we sit in the leadership chair. We realize how much depends on our abilities to do a good job. A lousy class sets a few students back. A failed research project may unwittingly add to the knowledge in a field. But a rotten leader spoils the contents of the whole barrel.

I believe that much of our success hinges not on our learned skills or methods, but on our character and the way it shapes our work. In speaking about character and good work in the same breath, I am drawing on an ancient and varied tradition that philosophers call "virtue ethics." Most famously associated with Aristotle, its strands are even older and are found in both Western and Eastern traditions. In broad strokes, a virtue ethics perspective takes excellence or flourishing as the aim of any human activity. It then associates that goal with a set of character traits—virtues—that lead to that end. In this way of thinking, acting like a good leader, being a good leader, and possessing the right leadership virtues are one and the same.

It may seem old-fashioned or odd to speak of virtues. It is kind of a dusty word. But the concept is as fresh as it ever was even as it travels under modern labels: core strengths, soft skills, character traits. Moreover, the term has the added benefit of highlighting that while some personality traits are morally neutral (being an introvert or an extrovert, for example), others (such as being honest or trustworthy) are intimately tied to ultimate values. Thinking about the aspects of ourselves that are connected to something larger can inspire us to do our work with greater passion and effect.

Getting a handle on the leadership virtues, in other words, promises to make your work more satisfying and help you do a better job. Many of the worries of new leaders and much of the advice they receive focus on the practical skills and duties of their new role. But the women in my seminars are interested in a set of deeper questions. They recognize that their leadership work both draws from and develops their core sense of self. They see that their internal struggles, values, and aspirations shape the way they put their skills into practice and perform their duties. They want to develop as human beings as much as they want to develop as deans or vice presidents. For me and for these women, a virtue ethics framework is resonant and speaks to this deep desire to connect work and inner self.

As I noted above, there is a long tradition of seeking to identify the virtues of effective leadership. One of the oldest and best comes from Sun Tzu's *The Art of War*, where the good commander is said to exhibit the following core virtues:

wisdom
sincerity
benevolence
courage
strictness (or discipline)[7]

A modern list was created by Joanna Barsh and her collaborators based on their research into the character traits of remarkable women business leaders. Barsh refers to the list as "capabilities" and says that the best leaders are characterized by their disposition and talent for the following:

meaning
positive framing
connecting
engaging
managing energy[8]

Items from both lists have found their way into my work and into this book. Barsh's list has been particularly influential in helping me understand the ways that the emotional and psychological work of leadership draws on virtues that can be honed and valued. We often dismiss a woman's abilities to connect, engage, and motivate as simply her nature or her inherited feminine traits. In taking these things seriously as virtues and as attributes that enhance leadership, Barsh and her coauthors lift up these ways of being and remind us to notice and celebrate them for the hard-won traits that they are.

Being an academic leader is something like preparing soldiers for battle or leading an empire—the models of leadership that interested Sun Tzu. And it is also similar to heading a complex business unit like the ones led by the women in Barsh's study. So both Sun Tzu and Jo-anna Barsh offer virtues worth considering for academic leaders. Despite the 2,500 years and the vast contextual differences that separate them, they share an emphasis on the relationship a leader must have with those whom she would lead. Trust, care, communion, shared purpose—these are parts of both lists, as are the subtle deployment of experience, vision, and wisdom.

I encourage the women in my seminars to think of how Sun Tzu's virtues apply to some of their current headaches, the problems that are keeping them up at night or driving them up a wall during the day. Is there a place for greater courage here? for a deeper sincerity? Might a better balance be found between benevolence and strictness? Taking Barsh as a guide to virtue yields different but equally valuable questions. Has your framing of the problem limited your ability to resolve it? How can you connect the problem to the larger purpose of your institution? Where are you failing to engage or energize others?

To their lists, I also would add a virtue that is particularly apt for academic life, especially for those charged with leading the faculty. This is the virtue of attunement, the intimate connection to the mood of a group.

A faculty is not a team or a committee. It is not a unit, a tribe, or a battalion. Like these other forms of human collaboration, a faculty is composed of individuals interacting according to spoken and unspoken rules. And like these others, when well led the faculty will function effectively in ways that promote the flourishing of its members and the larger organization.

But a faculty is less hierarchical than these other groups. And it is, by definition, composed of professors and not soldiers or representatives or businesspeople. Its members value autonomy and free thought. Many identify as critics or opponents of institutional structures. Even the most engaged among them is absorbed first in a disciplinary identity and only secondarily as a member of a particular faculty. There is tremendous respect for disciplinary expertise, and each member has experience in judging and being judged against a harsh standard. Faculty members are suspicious of empty talk, of metaphors uncritically imported from other arenas, and of those who would trade the known satisfactions of teaching and research for the ambiguous pleasures of administration. They are masters of analysis, wanting both means and ends held up to scrutiny. These traits make them good at being faculty members. This is why we want to put student minds in their care. It is why we trust the research they produce. But it is also why it is so difficult for a faculty to act collectively and toward a common good. It is why a faculty both needs and resists having a great dean.

When an academic leader is attuned to her campus, she understands its subtle energies—the way a disturbance in one small corner can ricochet or be subtly turned toward a higher purpose. She knows the meaning of the unexpected group gathered over tea in the faculty lounge, of the surprising agreement of sworn enemies on a curricular proposal, of the crossed arms on this one or the smile on that one's face in a meeting. She can read the way the faculty's energies rise and fall, the cycle of student passions, and the waves of alumni engagement.

The attuned leader treats each member of her community as an individual, but she is aware of the campus as a whole, as a complex organism whose movement depends on more than any of its parts. And she understands that each of the individuals that comprise it are both essential to the whole and utterly independent of it.

Such attunement allows her not only to predict but to shape behavior, encouraging a butterfly to flap its wings in one spot to put in motion small effects that build over time, creating renewal and change. She builds committees that can both deliberate *and* decide. She appoints leaders who are themselves attuned.

The well-attuned leader can shape her campus with carrots and only occasionally needs to use sticks. She can spot trouble before it starts and gauge which battles are worth fighting. She can help each faculty or staff member find a way to serve the college that suits their talents and interests.

Putting It into Practice

The practice of leadership requires focused attention on the processes by which change is made. It also requires a deep understanding of your institution—its culture, its business model, and its mission. Since change is always uncomfortable, learning to tolerate and even embrace that discomfort will help you inspire change and lead with greater efficacy.

REFLECTION QUESTIONS

How does being a woman affect my leadership style?

How would I define my institution's mission, business model, and culture?

Are they in alignment? If not, what needs to change?

What changes am I in the midst of leading?

At what stage of change is each of the projects?

How do I measure my strengths as a leader according to Sun Tzu's virtues? according to Barsh's?

Am I attuned to my campus?

What are some ways I can become a better leader?

Who can I ask for help as I work on my leadership skills?

5

Crafting a Vision

———

ONCE, AFTER a particularly raucous and disappointing faculty meeting where I discovered that the faculty was planning to do the exact opposite of what I—their provost and purported leader—had advised, I came home and told my husband that I felt like Moses must have when he stumbled down from the mountain and discovered the Israelites worshiping a golden idol. My husband kindly sidestepped the hubris of my analogy and asked, What did Moses do next? What did he do after that? And then what? What did he do for those mythic forty years that made him a good leader?

I knew his leadership wasn't about speed or a strong sense of direction. The distance the Israelites crossed was short. They could have gotten there much sooner. When I looked closely at the text, I saw that what Moses did, again and again, was offer the people a vision of the promised land. He kept reminding them where they had been (you were slaves in Egypt) and where they were headed (you will be a people of G-d). Over and over, the story describes the people giving up or complaining about the stresses of the journey. Each time, Moses held up a detailed vision of what was ahead. Without that vision of a better future, despair would have won.

I had failed because I hadn't offered a compelling vision. Some of our faculty didn't believe we could build a better curriculum. Others believed but weren't inspired to act. Still others were afraid that the curriculum I was describing was too far removed from where we were and would create a learning environment in which they wouldn't have a home.

In a business context, perhaps I could have fired the recalcitrant faculty or threatened them into compliance. But colleges are built on shared governance. Faculty have a meaningful role in setting the curriculum. Even if I had wanted to play hardball, my options were limited. If I wanted to see change, I would have to lead. If I wanted action, I would have to inspire it.

The key to inspiring change is to articulate a compelling vision. In his book *The Artist's Journey*, author and screenwriter Steven Pressfield describes how impressed he was the first time he spent time on a movie set and saw the countless decisions a director has to make. He says: "I used to marvel at how the director could answer so many questions from so many people so quickly and with such authority. . . . How did the director do it? How did he always know?" The director told him that the secret was that he "had a point of view."[1]

This artistic point of view—the selected approach to the film's subject, voice, and style—is analogous to a leader's vision. When you see the big picture and know the contours of the future you are hoping to create, the day-to-day decisions become easier. The right answer is the one that gets you closer to realizing your vision.

A movie can have a lot of writers, multiple stars, and a host of producers. But it can only have one director. The coherence and strength of the director's vision are what allow everyone else a chance to shine as individuals and to come together for a shared purpose. As a leader, you are taking on the role of director. Your unique point of view and vision will shape the direction in which the institution moves.

As I discussed in the previous chapter, I see our institutions as resting on three pillars: mission (Why do we exist? What is our end goal?), culture (How do we treat people? How do we get things done?), and business model (Where does the revenue come from? What do we spend it on?). Institutions work well when these three pillars are in alignment, and they fail when the alignment gets out of whack. If the mission outpaces the budget, the institution runs into financial trouble. If the institution is bringing in revenues, but the culture is toxic, people will stop caring about the mission. If it is has a positive culture but lacks a substantial mission, the institution won't be able to attract financial resources. And so on. Your vision paints a picture of a fully aligned future.

A Working Definition of Vision

Companies sometimes try to capture a leadership vision in a single sentence. For example, the Ford Motor Company's vision is "people working together as a lean, global enterprise to make people's lives better through automotive and mobility leadership." The vision at the Norfolk Southern Railway is to "be the safest, most customer-focused and successful transportation company in the world." Avon's vision is "to be the company that best understands and satisfies the product, service, and self-fulfillment needs of women—globally." The clarity of these three examples is admirable, as is the way that each recognizes the importance of all three pillars.

College communities, however, are less likely to embrace such succinct and direct statements of vision since from an academic standpoint they can appear facile and overly simplistic. Faculty, in particular, are likely to bristle at anything that sounds too much like a marketing slogan. As an academic leader, your vision will likely be framed in a more subtle and complicated way. But whether the vision is stated directly or indirectly, it has to do the work of inspiring change. Here's how I define it:

A leadership vision is a cluster of metaphors, concepts, stories, and images that point to a future that feels at once strange and familiar and that is clearly better than the present. It, thus, inspires action, creation, and engagement.

When I say that a vision has to be both strange and familiar, I am thinking of what is needed to inspire action. If the vision is too close to the way things are now, it won't have the heft that it needs to be truly inspiring or to really make a difference. But if it is too strange, too far from the current reality, it will leave people feeling abandoned: they won't be able to visualize themselves as part of the world you want to bring about. No one wants to create their own obsolescence. You can't expect anyone to embrace a future that doesn't include them or that includes them in a way that feels limiting or dismissive of their values and talents.

Imagine if the Ford vision included a hope that the company would automate all of its processes. How dispiriting that would be to its workers. Or imagine if a new Avon CEO announced that the company would no longer center the needs of women. I am sure that many of its employees would feel betrayed. On the other hand, when an Avon leader brought a new vision of becoming a company that served women beyond North America and across the globe, that was just strange enough to be inspiring and to motivate action.

Your vision is a response to your problems. It reveals what makes your institution uniquely situated to thrive. It explains who will be drawn to you and why. The visionary leader is appropriately bold. She invites us to do more than to merely mirror what is already so or even what can be seen just over the next hill. If others can see it clearly and fully already, then she hasn't aimed high enough.

The leader's vision has to inspire action and commitment. It has to be broad enough that each member of the community can fill in the details and find their place within it. They have to believe she sees it and believe she can take the institution there.

What a Vision Is Not

A vision is not the same thing as a goal. A goal is supposed to be clear, measurable, and achievable: losing twenty pounds, offering a more flexible curriculum, taking a trip to Paris. But a vision has to be more than that. It has to allude to a transformation and an end state that encompasses your deepest hopes and engages all of your senses: an image of the lightness of your body as you energetically stand at the peak of a mountain, the student who graduates having found her true calling, the way your mind broadens as you order a café au lait amid the bustling Parisian streets. The difference between a goal and a vision is the difference between heading toward a set of map coordinates and heading toward the promised land or the land of milk and honey.

A vision is also not purely a figment of the imagination. A leader has to be firmly grounded in reality. She has to see a future that can be attained and moreover that can be attained by starting from exactly where the institution already is. The ability to create a wholly new business or college does no good at all in this context. That is the role of the writer or utopian philosopher. A leader who sees too much of what isn't there won't have the skills that are needed to lead from one state to another.

Finally, visionary leaders are not prophets. A prophet demands change and repentance, but she does so by looking to the past, not the future. She urges a return to the days of old and orients herself toward the remembered past. The visionary leader is not returning her community to Eden. She is not nostalgic about how things used to be better. In fact, she eschews nostalgia for the past except as it reflects a commitment to values that can be reincarnated and transformed into a new future.

Finding Your Vision

It can be overwhelming to realize that you can't import a cookie cutter vision. A strong vision can't be purchased or outsourced to a consultant. A vision isn't so much discovered as it is created.

Your vision should be a mirror that reflects the very best possible state of your organization. What do you see that is so good it should be magnified? be made into a standard operating procedure? become your motto? The way you answer those questions will reveal your vision. At first, it will likely feel inchoate. It might start as a feeling you get on campus or when you talk with a specific employee. Pay attention to the contents of your daydreams and your actual nighttime dreams. Developing a vision is a creative project, and it therefore can't happen on a rigid timetable or a set schedule. Prepare for it as you would for any innovative process—by making time to muse and reflect, by engaging in lively conversation with creative friends, and by listening to your heart as well as your head.

When I first became president of Austin College, my dreams kept returning to images of the beautiful tall trees that line the campus's center walkway. And a single phrase, "roots and branches," flooded my mind every time I thought about the college. As I let myself meditate on these images and words, I realized that I had uncovered an important aspect of what the college needed to be: a place that draws strength from its past, its roots, and at the same time reaches its branches toward a new future. That became the organizing principle for our first strategic plan, and it was the foundation on which I built a vision for our future.

My friend George Parker is a consultant who works with executives across Europe, helping them create change in their organizations.[2] As an aid to vision development, he encourages the executives to imagine what he calls a "future memory." To do this, he suggests, picture the day you leave the job. How will your institution be different than it is now? What will you be most proud of? What fond memories will you have at that point? Let yourself imagine all of this in detail. I have found this to be an extremely beneficial exercise, and I use it to help me think about how I can best shape not only a large-scale vision, but smaller events and meetings as well. By starting with what I want to remember, I have a better sense of what I need to ensure happens.

When Vision Goes Astray

I've known presidents who are fearful of their own visions because they are unsure if their ideas can be realized. Those leaders stay too close to the "what is," managing budgets and personnel and alluding to a vision only rarely. If they are good managers and if the fates keep the revenues flowing, these presidents can last a long time in office.

I have also known leaders who announce a vision as soon as they land on campus. These are usually people who are more focused on the kind of leader they are than on the kind of institution they are leading. They bring the same vision to whatever institution will have them rather than crafting a vision suited to the individual context. These presidencies are usually short-lived because the mismatch between the president's focus on her predetermined plan and the campus's inherent strengths become more and more visible. Presidents with this style are usually forceful and often charismatic. Sometimes, they are able to land at another institution and try to fit the same garment on this next campus. I know one president who has tried out his pet vision on three different institutions.

Another mistake some presidents make is to speak as though the college was rudderless or without visionary leadership before they arrived. In both of my presidencies, I have been fortunate to follow long-serving presidents who developed compelling visions for the institutions. While each new presidency is an opportunity for a new vision to take hold, I was able to take the time to craft my vision from a position of strength and in dialogue with what had come before me. Each of us affects a finite piece of the institution's history, and it is wise to remain mindful that your institution has both a before and an after you. This fact should be both humbling and inspiring.

It is important to make sure that the vision you present is not so directive that others can't shape it. Not only are people more committed to something they help create, but the vision itself will be stronger if multiple voices add to its basic core. When I articulate a vision, I want it to be fecund so that the members of my community can plant their own seeds in its fertile soil.

Timing

Unfortunately, the question of a vision is usually asked too soon, sometimes before the president has even seen the campus. It isn't uncommon for a search committee to ask prospective candidates about their vision. While it is wise to expect that a newcomer will have an initial set of impressions and an idea of some of the ways the institution might need to evolve, a genuine vision takes time to percolate. It requires immersion in the culture of the organization and interaction with its people. The best visions are those that emerge collaboratively and with a full understanding of the organization's mission, culture, and business model. I have made the mistake of answering the vision question too soon, and it has usually meant I said things that weren't fully formed, or I was so vague to not really say much at all. Early on, it is better to shift the conversation to your immediate impressions and to the things you want to learn about the organization than to prematurely describe a vision.

Because the visioning process is creative, it requires you to get outside of operational mode. For me, that means I need first to unwind and then to get into my creative mindset. I do that faster when I spend time on something creative but unrelated—reading for pleasure, visiting an art gallery, seeing a new city. Those are the things that take me out of my everyday transactional mindset and allow new thoughts to arise. Once I have the beginnings of an idea, I often use my husband or another trusted friend as a sounding board and interlocutor.

Creativity

Crafting a vision is the most artistic part of leadership. It requires ingenuity and imagination. If you are going to do it well, you will have to find time for the kind of open-ended thinking that leads to new ideas.

My husband is a professional sleight-of-hand magician. He and his friends structure their days very differently from mine. When he is developing new material, he needs to retreat to his studio. As an artist, he has to make sure his schedule has big blocks of uninterrupted time so he can live with a creative problem and take advantage of the insights that arrive unexpectedly. He works on and dreams and thinks about a specific challenge (a new technique, the right words for a script, a technical challenge in a routine) until he has solved it. I remember this way of living from my time as a professor and scholar.

In contrast, my days are often filled end to end with short meetings and planning periods. Much of what I do is collaborative. I have to be able to move seamlessly from a budget meeting to a reception, from solving a personnel crisis to announcing a major gift, and from thinking to action. I rarely am able to spend more than a few hours at a time on a single issue.

So I guard my creative time fiercely. I block it out on my calendar, and I take advantage of weekend mornings to write and think. I also keep a notebook with me at all times so when inspiration arrives I can capture it for later review and analysis.

A genuine vision for your institution can't be generated from a distance. It takes deep knowledge of the culture, the mission, and the business model. You have to live inside the institution for a while if you are to identify its strange but better future.

I recommend resisting early calls to state your vision. Respond instead by talking about the questions you want to ask or the problems you want to solve. Restate the things that attracted you, and name the things that you are learning. Presuming to know exactly where the college should head when, as a newcomer, you have so much to learn is a way to get off on a very wrong foot.

What you should do early on is to make use of your "outsider within" status to reflect back aspects of the present that may be invisible to people with longer tenure. What strikes you as unusual? How does the way the college describes itself differ from what you see? What is the most exciting thing you have learned? What is the most troubling? What is your initial summary of the mission? the culture? the business model? Do they seem healthy? Are they in alignment?

These reflections set the stage for you to develop a vision. Equally important, this approach begins to give your community a sense of how you think and what you will lift up as important.

As you meet students, faculty, staff, alumni, and community members, you can present your sense of what you see as a series of hypotheses and invite these more seasoned members of the college to respond. You will learn a lot from what meets resistance and what is taken up as a helpful insight. You might say, for example, "I am surprised to find that the faculty doesn't do any advising. Why do you think that is?" Or "I am amazed at how robust the transfer population is. How does that seem from a student perspective?"

The most important things you are aiming to understand are what needs to change and what should never change. You are working to define the "problem" with where the institution is right now.

Engaging Others

Within the first year, you should develop a good sense of the institution's current state. It is important at this point to be able to succinctly summarize the key challenges and your sense of direction. You will want to begin sharing your thinking with as many audiences as possible. You still need confirmation that you are on the right track, and you definitely want as many constituents as possible to feel heard and understood.

You and your board should be in general agreement about direction. Are you laying the groundwork to expand? Will you be redirecting the mission? Is the campus culture in need of change? Do you want to attract a different type of student? You aren't ready at this point to lay out a ten-point plan, but you can begin to talk in ways that set the stage for the need to change.

In both my presidencies, I found it helpful to develop a few slides focused on the finances of the college that I could share with multiple audiences. It is reassuring to faculty and staff to know that they are seeing the same information as the trustees. The goal of these slides is to show the challenges to the college's financial model and to lay the groundwork for changes to how the college generates revenue. Showing the same slides over and over again helps to create a shared sense of the challenges and the reasons that change is needed.

In addition to slides, you can begin to develop a vocabulary to support your vision. How can you talk about the college's mission in ways that are inspiring? What stories and anecdotes can you share that sum up what is best about your institution? Who can you lift up as a model student or employee? What institutional accomplishments are most indicative of the vision?

This is a moment when the rhetorical leadership I described in the last chapter is particularly important. Every time you are asked to speak or to meet with someone, you have a chance to reinforce the groundwork for your vision.

Because we think about vision as a superpower, we tend to imagine it as a solo enterprise. The great leader crafts her vision in isolation and then announces it to a waiting community. There are leaders who operate like this—and it is often a disaster.

Much better is for the vision to be created in dialectic encounters with the community. You bring your hypotheses forward and then make changes and shifts as you come to understand the institution better.

In their book *Truth without Tears: African American Women Deans Share Lessons in Leadership*, Carolyn R. Hodges and Olga M. Welch warn against what they call "hacking" your way to a vision by trying to circumvent the collaborative process of building engagement along the way. They say, "The leader may believe that she possesses sufficient information to begin to develop an organizational vision. Confidently, she begins the work, often without consulting with enough internal stakeholders. . . . Without knowing them, she initiates actions that derail or delay the desired crafting of a viable vision."[3]

Working with a diverse team and making sure you are hearing a wide range of perspectives are crucial. As a president, you can easily surround yourself with people who always agree with you. Do not do this. Do everything you can to assure your team that you value divergent opinions. Do not kill the messengers who bring you bad news. Do not refuse to listen to constructive criticism.

Leaders have to be good communicators because a vision is hard to communicate. It can't be pointed to or displayed since by its very nature it doesn't yet exist. The leader has to translate her vision into words—concepts and metaphors—that can be taken up by others. It must be concrete enough and simple enough that it can live in minds beyond hers. But it has to be complex enough to feel new to those minds.

This puts a heavy emphasis on the leader's skills as a communicator. She needs to be a poet and a storyteller. This isn't only because we like stories. It is because stories are intrinsic to the nature of a vision. If it is spelled out too literally, it loses its power to inspire. Others can't take up a vision that is too concrete.

Sometimes, the people in your organization see that the current state of affairs isn't working. They know that change is needed. And sometimes, they are perfectly content and initially uninterested in a new future.

It can be tempting to think that one leadership situation is easier than the other. You might reason that if people are unhappy, they are looking for a new vision and will be eager to bring it about. Or you might confuse contentment with support for your vision and assume that a happy workforce will be eager to embrace something new. But in reality, no matter the initial state of your constituents, it will take time and effort for them to embrace a new vision. In an unhappy organization, you have to compete against cynicism. The people have already been let down. A past leader has failed them in some way. You have to work to build up enough trust for your vision to even be heard. In a happy organization, you have to fight complacency. Change is hard, and without the motivation of escaping pain, it is even harder.

Knowing the initial state of the community and its past experiences with embracing a vision of the future will help you determine how best to unveil your vision and the kind of resistance to expect. Don't be lulled into believing that you won't face resistance at all.

Strategic Planning

When you arrive in a new position, you are often asked to develop a strategic plan—either for the entire institution or for your unit. My phone rings often with questions about how to do this. In responding, I aim to demystify strategic planning.[4]

For a strategic plan to be "strategic," it must be aimed at a vision of the sort I have described. The plan lays out what a better, more successful version of your institution would be like, how it would operate, what it would achieve for students. For a strategic plan to be a "plan," it must give realistic general guidance for how to achieve that vision.

Many so-called strategic plans fail on one or both of these counts. Some plans are visionless. They may spell out some goals (e.g., "be in the top twenty-five universities" or "achieve a higher Carnegie classification" or "balance the budget"), but the goals appear unmoored. How will achieving the goals fulfill the institution's mission? Are these goals important in themselves? What is the broader purpose the institution is seeking to serve? Some strategic plans fail to offer an actual plan. Instead, they are catalogs of things to be purchased or activities to be undertaken. They may read as a laundry list of departmental requests. Or they might offer nothing more than a restatement of an earlier vision or goals.

For me, the best and most useful strategic plans are brief (five to ten pages), clear, visionary, and able to serve as a guide for future decision-making. A plan should be resilient enough to anticipate various external circumstances and should be able to help leaders at every level decide how to best invest the resources of both time and money. It should inspire and also set a practical framework whereby success can be measured over time.

There is no single or best process for developing a strategic plan. One approach is to start with a core group (faculty, students, staff, and perhaps an alum or a trustee) to work with me to develop and flesh out a vision. We often begin with an environmental scan. Where are we now? What are our strengths and challenges? Answering these questions requires that we collect data internally by inviting stakeholders into the discussion through surveys, workshops, and focus groups. We also collect external data through market research, benchmarking, surveys, or focus groups with prospective students and campus neighbors. The data collection is an important first step. But by itself, it won't create a vision. The vision process has to occur through the kind of creative work I described above. The planning committee can help develop and shape your intuitions and also help you find meaningful stories, images, and words to convey your vision.

Once the vision is in place, the next step is to identify the overall strategy for achieving it as well as some broad tactics. These too should be tested for viability through both internal and external research.

In our current strategic plan at Rhodes, we envision what we call "the Rhodes edge": every student will graduate intellectually ready to tackle the world's hardest problems, career or graduate-school ready to advance in their field, and leadership ready to make an impact in their workplaces, their communities, and the world. Moreover, we envision achieving this while remaining a residential liberal arts college of approximately 2,000 talented undergraduates. Our core strategy for achieving the Rhodes edge has four components: to continue to build academic and creative excellence, to foster a culture of belonging, to ensure a transformative student experience, and to secure the financial future of the college. In each of these areas, we have identified some general tactics to move us closer to the vision and to help guide future decisions about priorities.

If you go to the Rhodes website and read the plan, you will note that I use slightly different terminology there than I am using in this chapter. That is because Rhodes has long spoken of its mission statement as its "vision." Rather than mess with that tradition, in the plan on the website I use the term "overall goal" to describe what I am here calling a vision and continue to use the term "vision" for what would in most places be called a statement of mission. The words you use are less important than the underlying concepts, and you should feel free to adopt your terminology to your institution and context.

Strategic planning may or may not be part of your responsibilities. But every leader should be engaging in strategic *thinking*. A plan is created every few years to guide decision-making. Strategic thinking is the everyday, all-the-time way that plans become real. Not everyone at the institution participates in writing the plan, but everyone can think strategically as they carry out their work.

To me, strategic thinking at its most fundamental means keeping the visionary end in mind at all times. Every decision from the momentous (Should we reduce staff in this department?) to the seemingly mundane (What should I say in my welcoming remarks for tomorrow night's alumni event?) should be made in terms of the desire to draw ever closer to the realization of the vision.

When I start with that end, not only do the individual decisions become easier, they become part of a whole. Over and over, I ask myself and members of my team to focus on strategy. What are you trying to achieve? What is the goal or purpose of this event? this meeting? this activity? Is this the best way to achieve that purpose? How does this purpose relate to our overall strategic vision and plan for the college?

The more inclusive and engaging the strategic planning process, the deeper down in the institution these questions can be asked and answered. In an ideal world, every employee can see how their work fits into a bigger pattern and is part of the institution's strategic vision. So too can every alum, every donor, and even every student.

Thinking ahead about the process for gathering input and about how you will communicate during the strategic planning period is important. Ideally, you can provide a timeline and note key discussion points (with trustees, with faculty and staff, with students, and so on) at the beginning. This will help you stay on track and also help engage your community.

I sometimes joke that the ideal timeline for a planning process is one in which the board members are tapping their toes and wondering why it is taking so long, and the faculty members are astounded by how quickly it is unfolding. In practice, an institution-wide planning process will likely take most of a year. Planning for an individual unit can usually be accomplished in a semester. These time frames give room for research and consultation but don't allow for endless debates or distractions.

Putting It into Practice

A leadership vision, as defined above, inspires action, creation, and engagement. Building this vision is essential work and should be both pleasurable and exciting. My three-pillar model invites you to consider the ways you can align the mission, business model, and culture of your program or institution. Defining your vision allows you to steer past resistance and engage others in a positive future. It animates what can otherwise feel like a dry strategic planning process. Crafting a leadership vision is one of the most important and creative things you do. Take the time required to give it your full attention and skill.

REFLECTION QUESTIONS

What sparks your creativity?

How comfortable are you with uncertainty and risk?

What kinds of teammates do you want on your visioning and planning committee?

Which communication methods are most natural to you? At which ones can you get better?

How can you build experience in strategic planning?

Who can you turn to for advice and support as you craft your vision?

What are the most meaningful stories you tell about your institution?

What are the key symbols and images that represent the best of your institution?

How can you build on these stories and images to define a vision for the future?

6

Building Your Skills

ALTHOUGH I HAVE emphasized the inner work of preparing for and engaging in leadership, there are specific external skills and experiences that are important to have. The women in my seminars are at various stages in their careers, and so they come with a wide range of current roles and types of responsibilities. Almost all of them wonder if they are learning the things they need in order to move up in their careers. In this chapter, I offer advice about some basic skills that are expected at almost every midlevel and senior academic leadership position.

It can be frustrating when you need to develop in an area, but your current position doesn't offer much room for you to learn. In my work with various women over the years, we have found creative ways to get experience outside of the constraints of a particular job description. I share these tips as well. The second part of the chapter focuses on a few advanced skills, particularly those that are required for the presidency.

The best way to put yourself in line for a more senior position is to perform your current work with excellence. I call this "growing where you are planted." Gaining a reputation for being an outstanding faculty member, a brilliant coach, a successful gift officer, or a transformational student affairs professional makes it easy for people to see you in a more senior role. Your early experience will continue to inspire confidence over the long term. Those whom you lead will appreciate that you once walked in their shoes and know from the inside what their work is about.

In order to be considered for senior leadership positions, and certainly to be competitive in national searches, you need to demonstrate facility in areas that can be challenging to experience in the earlier stages of your career. The basic competencies that matter most are budget responsibility, revenue responsibility, personnel responsibility, and fund-raising experience.

Budget Responsibility

Many lower-level positions don't give you authority to manage a budget. You may be responsible for small amounts of institutional funds—managing your own travel or research account, for example—but this isn't the same thing as creating an annual budget plan, moving it through the institutional approval process, and then spending the allotted money properly and well during the course of the year. Having this broader budgeting experience is important because it reveals that you can be trusted to steward institutional resources and because you develop savvy about the way money is accounted for and distributed.

How can you get this experience if you haven't yet had it? In some fields, exposure to budget responsibility first comes through serving as the principal investigator on a research grant. Some faculty members are likely to first encounter budget responsibility when they become a department chair or a program director. Student affairs professionals may be given small sums to distribute for programming. And any faculty member might oversee a budget for a specific project or area of responsibility. If you are asked to take responsibility for making something happen—even if it is a relatively small thing, such as a staff retreat or a student-run project—I encourage you to treat the budget seriously.

Tell your supervisor that you would like to submit a budget plan and that you would like to work with the business office to establish an account for the project. You can explain that you are looking for broader experience in understanding the rules that govern institutional expenditures and also that it is important to you for the project to come in on budget. Even if you can't negotiate sign-off responsibility for the project account, treat it as though you have that formal responsibility by keeping track of the money using your institution's established categories.

Make an appointment with a budget officer and ask them to review your budget plan. They will help you understand the difference between restricted funds and operating funds and can give you an overview of what kinds of expenses can be charged to what kinds of accounts. At some colleges, money for alcohol or food has to come from special sources of revenue, for example. Some money is fungible, meaning you can move it from one purpose to another, while other money has to be used for a specific purpose. The aim here is to learn what these differences are and how they matter. You are also looking to gain practice in effectively using the institution's money and responding to challenges that emerge. You want to learn what to do when one part of the project costs more than anticipated. And you want to practice making financial decisions that have consequences—even if you're only deciding whether to go with a more expensive set of folders or not. You do not need responsibility for a large budget in order to learn these things or in order to be able to talk about what you have learned when you are preparing for a promotion.

You should find that the budget officers are glad to offer you advice and tutoring. Their chief complaint is that others in the institution are indifferent to spending rules and pay no attention to overages. They are likely to appreciate that you want to be an ally in taking wise care of your budget. Learning to speak their language and use the approved budgeting software will make it easier for you to assume greater amounts of fiscal responsibility. You can develop a reputation as someone who plays by the financial rules and can be trusted.

Budget authority gives you some internal power that can be used to build relationships with colleagues. Think about the way that your expenditures might be of use to someone else. If, for example, you are planning to purchase markers that will be used by your workshop participants for a day and then no longer needed, you could call a colleague in student life and ask if they would be interested in the markers when your conference ends. You might even invite them to join you in choosing the type of marker so that your purchase best serves your needs and theirs. Using a small portion of your budget to buy coffee or lunch for a colleague who is assisting you or whose advice could be helpful to your project is another nice way to build up goodwill, encourage participation, and consolidate support for what you are doing. In academic affairs in particular, making savvy use of the wine-and-cheese budget helps to develop buy-in.

Revenue Responsibility

Budget control is one important aspect of fiscal management. You are learning to spend institutional money. But there is another side to finances that is in some ways even more important for senior leaders: revenue creation. Most dean and vice presidential positions carry expectations about forecasting and earning revenues. In the case of admissions and development, the abilities to accurately forecast revenues and to achieve set goals are essential to the role. But deans and vice presidents of student affairs typically have responsibility for forecasting housing or dining revenues, and provosts and academic deans may have responsibility for generating revenues through adult education, study abroad programs, conferences, or external research funding.

Forecasting is tricky and is therefore an important skill to add to your toolbox. It is essentially the ability to accurately predict how much revenue an endeavor will generate. Your institution is likely to want revenue targets to be ambitious enough that everyone is motivated to work hard to achieve them and at the same time realistic enough that budgets and plans can be made on their basis. Learning what is expected in this area is essential. Once your forecast has been accepted as part of the college's budget, you are responsible for actually generating that revenue. The college is now counting on the success of your initiative, and if you cannot bring in the planned revenue, you could create a budget deficit. Sometimes, your revenues and expenses are tied together—for example, if you have to spend a certain number of dollars per conference attendee. In that case, lower revenues may correlate with lowered expenses, and a deficit is avoided. But it is rare that the correlation works exactly, so you need to take the revenue projection seriously. Demonstrating that you have had experience forecasting and then meeting or exceeding revenue goals is important as you advance in your career.

While you are mastering the skills associated with revenue generation, you must also learn how to cope with the stress that such responsibility brings. As a classroom professor or entry-level administrator, your errors or failures affect you personally and perhaps are upsetting to a small group of students or colleagues. But there are rarely serious consequences for you or others. Misjudging how much material you can cover in a class or semester, for example, doesn't bring much in the way of significant problems. But misjudging revenue targets creates an immediate budget problem, and your mistake will need to be acknowledged and made up for by others who have exceeded their own revenue goals or by a reduction of expenses someplace within the college.

People can lose their jobs if key targets are missed and overall revenues can't support overall expenses. Programs or financial aid to deserving students might be cut. This is a heavy responsibility, and learning to live with the weight of it is part of the leadership path. Leadership is stressful in large part because the decisions you make have real consequences for you and for others. Those who might hire you for senior positions will want to know that you have found ways to manage this kind of stress and that you are not paralyzed by it.

Personnel Responsibility

A third area where it is crucial to gain early experience is managing other employees. Learning to be the boss of someone is a bumpy road. Unlike budgets, which sit quietly waiting for you to address them, people run on their own schedules and have their own priorities and personalities. One specific skill for which hiring committees will be on the lookout: have you had the authority to hire and fire? Responsibility for appointing, overseeing, supporting, coaching, leading, and evaluating others becomes more intense the more senior your position.

If you are at the beginning of your career, this kind of personnel experience can be hard to get, and you may think that it is unlikely that you are going to have a staff assigned to you. But you can gain experience by treating all of your supervisory experiences with seriousness and attention. Even if your only opportunity at this point is the oversight of student workers or student research assistants, you can take their appointment, evaluation, and (if necessary) termination as seriously as you would any other responsibility. Make these appointments with care, recognizing that you are turning institutional responsibility over to the person you hire. Aim to clearly specify your expectations and create a process for ongoing evaluation and feedback. Take seriously the concept of yourself as the boss—not only in having a certain amount of power but in being the guide and leader for those reporting to you.

Just as you learn by building relationships with budget officers, you gain a great deal of wisdom by partnering with the human resources professionals on your campus. They can explain the written policies that apply to various job categories as well as review your legal and institutional obligations as a supervisor.

In my experience, faculty members often have a great deal of difficulty making this transition in identity. As professors, we experience ourselves largely as independent agents; we work with a department chair and dean, but we aren't really their employees. There is a casual style of communication between faculty members that obscures the extent to which the department chair is, or should be, taking responsibility for the work and the development of the faculty members in her department. Thus, having little experience of being an employee, it can be challenging for a professor to learn how to effectively become a boss. In an interview for a more senior role, you are likely to be asked about how you manage people, and you should be able to give an answer that demonstrates confidence with this role.

Fund-Raising Experience

Raising funds for your institution can be the most difficult area in which to gain opportunity and experience because it is not something anyone should attempt without clear authorization. It might seem as though there is no harm in asking someone to make a donation in support of your project or program, but there are several ways this could be disastrous. One problem is that the donor may already be part of a larger institutional fund-raising plan. There is little that is more frustrating for a president or an advancement vice president than being told that a million-dollar prospect has just been asked for a $5,000 gift. Freelance fund-raising upends efforts to coordinate fund-raising across the institution and produces weaker results.

Even if you are sure that the prospective donor isn't otherwise part of the institution's fund-raising plan, in asking for a gift, you are making a statement about the institution's most important priorities. Without explicit authority to speak on behalf of the college as a whole, you are offering a potential misrepresentation to the donor. Finally, your institution has many policies governing how gifts are requested, accepted, acknowledged, counted, and managed. Without familiarity with these rules, you could find yourself in trouble for mismanaging money.

In sum, do not run off and try to raise money on your own. But how then can you gain experience in fund-raising? The first step is to figure out who does the fund-raising in your institution. Sometimes, this work is completely centralized, and all of it is done through the president and the office of advancement. At other places, individual deans, department chairs, athletic directors, or coaches have responsibility (within limits) for fund-raising. Build a relationship with one of these people. Ask them to explain the cycle that drives giving (cultivation, asking, stewardship) and share their experiences with you. Understanding the theory behind fund-raising is as important as learning how to actually ask for money. If you are fortunate, someone will take you to a donor meeting, and you will be able to see these steps in action.

If you are part of a program or project that is funded by a donor, see if you can be involved in thanking them or inviting them to see the results of their gift. Spending time with donors allows you to understand their motivations and will help you structure gift opportunities in the future.

You can also keep an eye out for prospective donors. Perhaps there is someone who attends all of the lectures sponsored by your department, or perhaps a former student just got a big promotion and wrote to tell you how much your class was a factor in her success. Sharing this information with the development officers will be helpful. They might even ask you to stay connected and assist in creating a giving opportunity.

Any or all of these experiences will allow you to say yes when you are asked during an interview if you have had experience with fund-raising.

Assessing Your Basic Skill Set

As you consider your career opportunities and goals, look for ways that you can gain experience in the four core areas I have identified: budget responsibility, revenue responsibility, personnel responsibility, and fund-raising experience. Just as important, reflect on these experiences as you have them. Draw lessons each semester from your work in these areas. Think hard about what you are learning in terms of actual procedures and skills but also in terms of your broader sense of your own abilities and strengths. What personal or spiritual growth can you identify? What are the conditions under which you do your best and worst work? Who can serve as a model for good practices in these areas?

This kind of serious reflection and the resulting ability to speak articulately about your professional style and strengths will serve you well. Such self-examination can also serve as a blueprint for your next steps or to inspire you to take on a new kind of project.

Advanced Skills

Moving into a vice presidency or a presidency requires an even more advanced set of skills. The *Chronicle of Higher Education* published a substantial report on the essential skills that are required of college and university presidents:

1. The ability to analyze your institution's business model to lead change while staying true to your core mission
2. The ability to innovate and take smart risks that don't jeopardize day-to-day operations
3. The ability to foster positive relationships with a diverse set of constituents, on campus and beyond
4. The ability to develop a 21st-century communications strategy
5. The ability to prepare for and manage a campus crisis or scandal[1]

This is a fascinating list. One thing to note is that there is nothing here about teaching or learning. There is nothing here that speaks in favor of a president who is a professor or who has spent her career in the academy. There is nothing here about understanding the norms of academic culture, academic freedom, or shared governance. Nor is there anything connected to knowledge of how learning occurs or what outcomes a college education should provide. Perhaps these university-specific skills are assumed, but nevertheless the college president of the future would seem to be much less an academic powerhouse and much more of a savvy CEO.

While I would certainly emphasize the importance of an academic grounding and vision for a president, my sense is that the *Chronicle's* report is based on the important recognition that many of the assumptions that used to undergird higher education are no longer operating. Presidents now have to contend with serious strains on the business model, a disaffected public, and an imperative to make a college education both less expensive and more relevant. We have to contend as well with social media and the air of almost constant crisis on which it thrives. The ability to enact change—to develop a vision and a strategy and to lead—is becoming ever more crucial.

Based on this list, it might seem as though every effective president has to be a superwoman, equally able to master such diverse skills as emotional engagement and impersonal business analytics. There is some truth to that impression. The presidency is complex and draws on both left- and right-brain thinking and on both emotional and intellectual intelligence. But another truth about these advanced skills is this: the president does not have to single-handedly know everything there is to know about these things, but she needs to have the ability to build an effective team of experts on whom she can rely and with whom she will lead.

Leading any complex organization requires teamwork. Building a senior leadership group and keeping its members focused on institutional strategy are the essence of the advanced presidential skill set and the thing that distinguishes great presidents from those who are merely good enough.

Building a Team

When I hire a vice president, I look for someone who knows more about their area of responsibility than I do, who can work well with others, and who can balance strategic thinking with day-to-day implementation. I have been fortunate to work with several amazing senior leadership teams. Some of these individuals were hired by my predecessor, and many I hired myself. Making these appointments is in many ways the most impactful thing I do as a president, and I give the hiring process my full attention.

Randy Helm, president emeritus of Muhlenberg College, gave me two important pieces of advice: don't hire grouches, and you can't teach people to be smart. What makes this good advice—beyond ensuring that you don't wind up working with unhappy, slow thinkers—is that it is a reminder that character matters as much as skill set. The temperament, values, and personal characteristics of the members of your team set the tone for how each of their units function. The ways these people interact with others reflects on you as well as on the institution. You have to trust them to know their job and to have the skills to help you build and enact an overall institutional strategy. A personal connection also matters. These are people you will be spending time with when you are at your best and your worst.

Building a senior team isn't just a matter of hiring talented people. Those individuals have to function as a true team. This means that they must embrace a shared commitment to the entire institution and not merely to their unit. It also means that they respect each other's expertise, can debate effectively, and can build positive relationships with each other. Inevitably, we bring something of our own family dynamics to our working groups, so it is important for the president to be aware of the ways unconscious patterns can intrude. If you grew up in a family that kept secrets, that always had a good child and a bad one, or that spent time tiptoeing around an emotionally unstable parent, you have to be aware of not replicating those patterns of relating within your leadership team.

Group dynamics are complicated for another reason: the number of relationships in a group is significant. Each person can have a relationship with each other person, and there are multiple combinations of threes, fours, and so on. Each of these subgroups has to be healthy and constructive if the team is to function at its best. A good leader watches for tensions in the team as a whole and within any of its subsets. She works to ensure positive interactions at every level.

Loyalty is a subtle and significant aspect of good teamwork. No one should want team members who are loyal to a fault or who put personal commitments above the good of the institution. But within that scope, it does matter that your teammates are loyal to you. Knowing that they want you to succeed and that they are willing to do everything they can to help you makes your job easier and helps you be more effective. Good team members are loyal enough to even tell you the things you don't want to hear.

A new president found herself battling her institution's alumni after she made what seemed to be an inconsequential change to a long-held campus tradition. When she called me for advice, I wondered why her senior team hadn't stepped in to prevent her from making this rookie mistake. Why did they watch her make a misstep? She learned from this that building a genuine team gives vice presidents the courage to steer the president away from her own misguided ideas. Without that, she is left with a team of yes-people and has lost the benefit of loyal thought partners and external expertise.

Putting It into Practice

Skill development requires more than just putting in the famed 10,000 hours for mastery. In addition to time on task, it requires reflection on how that time is used, the examination of what can be learned from each experience, and the testing of new methods and hypotheses. Regularly setting aside time to analyze your skill development, set new goals, and try new ways of accomplishing things will help you develop faster. So, too, will getting regular feedback and insight from others.

REFLECTION QUESTIONS

Where am I in my skill development?

How can I create opportunities to practice new skills?

Who can advise or coach me on these next steps?

Who can I count on to tell me hard truths?

How adept am I at deploying the multiple skills required for senior leadership?

7

Winning the Job

———

AT LEAST ONCE a week, my phone rings with a query about the application process for a senior position. The questions arise at all stages of the search process: Is it the right time to apply? How do I prepare to succeed at an interview? How do I negotiate a contract? In this chapter, I offer a basic overview of the usual process as well as answers to these and other questions.

The search process for a senior position is often shrouded in mystery and is in many ways unlike the job application routes that a woman has already mastered. One central difference is that applying for deanships, vice presidencies, and presidencies almost always requires working with a third-party firm. Colleges use search firms for senior-level administrative hiring for three main reasons: to define the position, to build a strong candidate pool, and to serve as a liaison between the candidates and the college.

Defining the position is crucial and goes far beyond just listing the job title and the key areas of responsibility. To find the right person, the college leaders have to think about what they want the candidate to accomplish. What are the key challenges that the new hire will face? What are the priorities? What kind of experiences would indicate that the person could meet these challenges and accomplish these goals? What personal qualities are important for success?

We take it for granted that a vice presidential or presidential prospectus will include a list of desired personal characteristics, which is a reminder of just how different these jobs are from others on campus. In addition to skills, education, and experience, these positions' descriptions often demand particular character traits. A job ad for a professor of philosophy would never specify that the candidate needs a good sense of humor or should value complexity or be a good listener. But it is common to see these requirements and others like them in a senior-level prospectus.

A search firm consultant spends time with whoever is doing the actual hiring (the president for vice president and c-suite positions, the board for a president), with the search committee, and with multiple constituents on campus. Her goal is to help the campus coalesce around a shared understanding of the position and then write a prospectus to reflect that.

A prospectus also includes a positive—but ideally authentic—depiction of the college. Part of the search consultant's role is to build a pool of strong applicants. The expectation is that the best candidates already have great positions and may not be formally or openly on the job market. The prospectus should entice those people to consider this opportunity.

The search consultant does not rely on the prospectus to do the talking, however. She draws on her contacts and her knowledge of higher education to solicit candidates individually. Unlike a faculty search, which may yield dozens or even hundreds of qualified candidates, the pool of qualified senior executives is small. When I search for a vice president, I am thrilled if fifteen candidates can be found who truly meet the requirements and who are interested in the job.

The search consultant also serves a buffer between the college and the candidates. She can answer tough questions, gently deliver negative news, and talk up both parties to the other. This is one of her most important and useful roles. As a candidate, working with a search firm is a bit like working with a real estate agent when you are buying a house. She works for the college, so her ultimate loyalty is with them and not with you. But her goal is to make a successful match, and so she has every reason to be frank and helpful as you navigate the discernment and application process. Her reputation depends on making successful placements. Although your interests (as the applicant) are not exactly hers, you can count on her to want what is best for the ultimate match.

If you have been doing administrative work and moving up the ranks, you may have already gotten calls or notes from search consultants asking you to consider this or that opportunity. You may be perusing the ads in the *Chronicle of Higher Education*, at HigherEdJobs.com, or at DiverseEducation.com. Either way, a conversation with the search consultant is the most important first step in applying for a position.

Search consultants are an often untapped resource for advice about your career. The good ones have seen numerous successful and unsuccessful searches. They have talked with hundreds of applicants, and they have a good sense of what makes a competitive application package. They know the market better than anyone else, and they can help you figure out your place in it.

If you wonder if you are ready for a vice presidency or a presidency, a frank talk with a good search consultant can help you identify the strengths and weaknesses in your credentials and experience. You can also let her know the kind of positions you are looking for and ask her to keep you in mind if a potential match comes along. Relationships with search consultants develop over time. I was persuaded to apply for the presidency of Austin College by Tom Courtice, who had taken the time to get to know me and could see—even before I did—that this would be a good match. Similarly, Shelly Storbeck oversaw the searches that placed me at Muhlenberg College and then, many years later, at Rhodes College.

You can find the good consultants by looking at the job ads for the searches at the kinds of institutions at which you would like to work. You can also ask colleagues in senior roles about their experiences with the search consultants who placed them.

Sometimes, even for senior-level searches, the college will not use a professional search consultant. To continue the real estate metaphor, this is a bit like a house that is for sale "by owner." It may not be an absolute red flag, but it should certainly raise some questions in your mind. At this level, the norm is to use a search firm. This institution has made a conscious decision to head in a different direction. Is it to try to save money? Is it because the board doesn't like to ask for help? Is it because they already have an internal candidate? If you decide to apply, be aware that this is indicating potential risks, and see if you can get direct answers to these questions. Be aware, too, that without the participation of a search consultant, there may not be anyone who can answer these questions until you are already in the midst of the process.

Deciding Whether to Apply

The position prospectus is its own genre, and it is important to read it closely. You are looking at the whole picture and also looking for clues about what the situation at the college actually is and whether you would be happy working there. The language in the prospectus can help you see if they are looking for a change agent or someone who can continue on an already established path, for example. The committee worked hard on the search prospectus and likely every word was edited and reviewed at several levels of the institution. Take time to read it thoroughly and to think about the perspectives of those who developed it.

You should also look at the college's website. In addition to providing more about the institution overall, there is likely to be a page devoted to the search process. It might have the names of the members of the search committee, the search timeline, and notices to the campus about the general progress of the search.

As you think about whether to apply, you are assessing the position, yourself, and—most important—the potential for a match between you. Not getting a job you really want is disappointing. Taking a job you really don't want is disastrous.

In your initial conversation with the search consultant, you can ask about things that aren't covered in the prospectus. Good questions include:

Why is the position open?
You want to know if you would be stepping into a messy situation or if the transition is likely to be a smooth one. There is a difference between a position that is vacant because the incumbent retired or took a new job that is clearly a step up, and a job that is open because of a firing, death, or scandal. Your chances of success aren't hindered or helped either way, but you definitely want to know what you would be facing. If there was a problem with the previous officeholder, do your best to find out what it was. The search consultant might not be able to give you the details, but she should be able to provide a general assessment of the situation. She can also tell you if there is an interim person in the job and what else has been done to address whatever issues led to the opening.

Who makes the final decision, and what role will they play in the search process?
Here, you are looking to understand whether the actual decision-maker will be part of the search from the beginning or just come in at the end. When I hire a vice president, I chair the search committee because I want to demonstrate my commitment to the candidates from the beginning. Other presidents may prefer to let the committee identify two or three finalists and then choose from among them. In that case, you might not meet the president until near the end of the search. In a presidential search, the ultimate decision likely requires ratification by the entire board even though the members will be responding to a recommendation by the search committee.

Who is on the search committee, and how were they chosen?
The answer to this can tell you something about the culture of the college. A student representative on the committee lets you

know that student voices are valued. Elected faculty representation indicates a commitment to shared governance. The chaplain's presence tells you that the college's religious tradition matters. In a vice presidential search, it is helpful if there is at least one other vice president on the committee to help candidates get a sense of how the senior team works together. In a presidential search, the majority of the committee will be trustees.

What level of confidentiality can I expect?

It is typical for presidential searches to be completely confidential in order to encourage sitting presidents to apply. Some public institutions are required to make the names of their finalists known, however. Vice presidential searches are more likely to require finalists to spend a day on campus, and they are rarely completely confidential. Chief academic officer candidates will likely be expected to make a presentation to the faculty. Sometimes, the open presentations are even taped or streamed online. You want to know ahead of time how this will play out. The level of confidentiality is important to understand before you find yourself in the midst of a search.

Would I be the first woman (or first woman of color, first queer woman, and so on) in this position? Do the committee members seem open to that?

The search consultant wants to build a diverse candidate pool, but that doesn't mean the search committee is genuinely interested in considering you as a candidate. If you would be the "first" of any kind, I recommend being relatively direct with the consultant about her reasons for thinking that you could be hired and that you would be happy, if you were. Has the committee thought about this? discussed it? Has something at the college changed since the previous hire that makes it more likely that they would be prepared to welcome you? There were presidencies that initially seemed interesting to me but that I decided, as a Jewish woman, not to pursue because it was clear to me that the college was not prepared to hire a Jewish president, and I didn't want to waste my time. On the other hand, I was the first woman and the first Jewish president at two different institutions—both of which were indeed prepared and able to take this step.

What is the search timeline and process?

Typically, the consultant spends three months or so gathering candidates. The committee then identifies eight to ten candidates to interview at a neutral site (often called an airport interview). From that pool, two to four finalists are chosen, and their references are checked. Some subset of that group is then invited for an on-campus interview or for a more extensive interview at some other location. The entire process can take anywhere from a few months to nearly a year. There are many variations on the procedures and timeline, so asking for details will help you understand how the search committee is planning to move forward.

What is the salary range for the position?

Listen carefully to the answer to this question, and then believe it. The consultant will usually give a range or a sense of what she sees as the top of the institution's bracket. She will also want to know what you make now and what you are hoping for or expecting. You can give a general range as well. This isn't a time to game your responses. You are looking to see if this is a match, and salary is an important place where overlap has to occur. If the search consultant tells you that your expectations are outside the range of this institution, trust her. Don't assume the committee members will stretch once they see how wonderful you are. The range is likely set by the fiscal realities of that institution and its overall pay scale and not by the desire to lowball candidates.

Would they be able to agree to [my deal breaker]?

If you have a deal-breaker request, this is the time to mention it, and see if it can be on the table. Perhaps you would only take the job if it comes with tenure or meets a certain salary number or offers a position for your spouse or tuition for your kids. If there are things you want but that you could imagine taking the job without, you don't have to bring them up at this point. But if something is an absolute must-have, then let that be known as early as possible. There is no point in wasting your time or the search committee's time—and irritating the search consultant—by applying for a job that you know you won't take.

You should be generally prepared to take every job for which you apply. This doesn't mean you won't drop out of the search at some point because of something you learn along the way or because you don't feel the spark of connection with the search committee. But it does mean that applying for this kind of job is in itself a serious step. It isn't something to do just for the experience.

I recommend that you not apply unless you feel good about both the institution and the job based on what you read in the prospectus, what the search consultant has told you, and your web sleuthing. If you really can't begin to imagine yourself at this type of college or in that particular town or doing the actual work described in the prospectus, then you shouldn't apply.

I do not recommend applying as part of a plot to coax more money or a promotion out of your current college. Institutions spend significant money and time on these searches, and trying to game the system is not a good idea. The world of higher ed search consultants is a small one, and they wield enormous influence. You do not want to get a reputation as someone who sees the application process primarily as an opportunity to negotiate a better deal at home or as something to step into lightly.

Being an Internal Candidate

An internal candidacy requires special considerations. In higher education, it is unusual for there to be an internal appointment to the presidency. When it does happen, it might be because the institution has been in some crisis and needs the stability that a known person can bring or because the institution has a highly specialized mission. Internal promotions to vice president are more common.

As an internal candidate, you have an advantage in that you know the institution well and have a deep sense of its needs. The committee will rightly see that you could get started in the position without a lot of lead time. But these very strengths can also be perceived as weaknesses. Some committee members might worry that you have already formed alliances or won't be able to bring new perspectives to the institution. I sometimes think that higher education is a field where it is assumed that the devil you don't know is better than one you know.

Here are some questions to consider as you decide whether to become an internal candidate:

Are you are being urged to apply?

It is flattering to have colleagues asking you to apply for a senior position or telling you that you are a shoo-in. Enjoy this praise and appreciate it as a sign that you are doing your current job well. But before you leap into the search, it is important to reflect on how widespread this enthusiasm is. Is it coming from many directions or just from your friends? Is the eagerness tied to specific qualities or ideas you have, or is it grounded in anxiety about the unknown? Do your fans have a vision of what the job requires that matches your skills? Be aware that none of the people cheering you on have seen the other applicants. Their enthusiasm for you as a known person might evaporate when faced with the prospect of a seemingly more glamorous outsider. If people are suggesting you apply and you want the job, it is fine to ask them to formally nominate you. Multiple nominations are a sign to the search committee that you have a base of support.

Are you already doing the job?

If you are serving as the interim leader, you have a richer sense of what the job actually entails. Others have had a chance to see you in action and to understand what you bring to the position. This can give you a significant advantage in the search process. If you do go forward, it is important to think about the differences between your interim role and how you would approach the position if named to it more permanently. Perhaps you were asked to "clean house" as the interim leader and now need to show that you can provide more stable support for your team. Or perhaps your interim role was the exact opposite: you were asked to be a caretaker and just keep things humming along for a bit. If so, you have to work harder to demonstrate your skills as a change agent and leader.

Does the president or board chair support your application?

Before you apply, I recommend that you have a frank conversation with whoever is leading the search or making the hiring decision. You can tell them you are considering submitting an application and would like to know if they see you as a viable candidate. Make it clear you are not asking if you will get the job—but you are giving them a chance to veto you if they already know that they want to head in a different direction. You can explain that you do not need or expect a courtesy interview and expect to be evaluated by the same standards as other candidates. You can also say that you would appreciate being offered the opportunity to withdraw from the search if it becomes clear you will not be asked to move forward at some point. Demonstrating your openness to this kind of dialogue puts you in a stronger position, and asking to be kept informed allows for a graceful exit if necessary. The latter is also good for the institution since it preserves your dignity and allows you to continue to serve effectively in your current role.

Does the prospectus speak to your strengths?

It is important to read the prospectus with a critical eye. You are looking to see if it is written in a way that opens the door for an internal candidate (e.g., "a deep knowledge of the challenges facing Job U") or if the characteristics being sought point to the desire for an outside person (e.g., "the ability to bring new ideas and perspectives"). Be as rigorous in considering whether this position is a potential match as you would be if it were an opening at a different institution.

Are you prepared to be turned down?

Losing out on a job for which you applied is always disappointing. But when you are an internal candidate, it is also risky. You need to think carefully about the consequences of being known as a failed candidate. Will you remain in your current position? Will you seek opportunities elsewhere? It is particularly important to understand how confidential the search will be and how much public risk you will be taking by applying.

Has the initial search failed?

Sometimes, a failed search leads to an institution asking an internal person to apply at the last minute. If you are presented with this opportunity, be sure to get a clear sense of the expectations for the job and the reasons an external candidate could not be found. I know many successful vice presidents who were hired in this way, but the potential for failure has to be considered.

After thinking it through, if you decide to join the search as an internal candidate, you should prepare your cover story so that you can answer the questions you will be asked by your colleagues. It is helpful to have someone nominate you. Then you can say something along the lines of "I have been nominated and have let the search committee know that they may consider my credentials." Or you might decide that you are brave enough to be open about your desire for the position and actively campaign for it. Be aware, however, that academics tend to be suspicious of this kind of overt ambition.

How to Apply

The search consultant should explain what you need to do to be considered as a candidate. Typically, she wants your curriculum vitae and a cover letter.

If you are coming out of the faculty, I recommend rethinking your CV and adjusting for this type of search. You should center your leadership experience and accomplishments. In a typical faculty CV, there is a lengthy list of publications and then perhaps, toward the end, a list of committee service. But for leadership work, your scholarship is less relevant than the important initiatives you brought to life as chair of the college-wide curriculum committee. You need to find a structure for your CV that helps the reader understand your work as a leader and not just as a scholar or professor.

The cover letter should be relatively brief, no more than three pages. I aim for two. Your goal is to help the search committee picture you in the role. The committee members are focused on their campus and the job. You need to show them how you fit into that. Don't make them do the work of connecting your accomplishments to the job requirements. It is a common mistake to try to impress the committee with a list of the many amazing things you have done. It is better to stick to the things that are most relevant to the work described in the prospectus.

If you anticipate a major hurdle, it is better to address it directly. So you might write, "Although I have spent the last ten years at a small private college, my education and my earlier position at Big U have prepared me for the broad scope and mission of Open Job U. I am eager to return to this environment." Or, "Although I have spent my career in the Northeast, I have fond memories of visiting my grandparents every summer in the southern town that was their home. The pace of small-town living and the community feeling that can only be developed when one knows one's neighbors is very appealing to me."

Take time to get the tone right. It is difficult to write a letter that sounds appropriately humble while still touting your fitness for the position. The search consultant will often be happy to read your first draft and make suggestions about ways you can strengthen it. She has also seen hundreds of CVs and can guide you in ways to present yourself effectively. Don't hesitate to ask for advice on both the CV and the cover letter.

There are a few search firms in higher ed that have a more corporate practice and approach. They tend to do most of the initial vetting themselves and present the search committee with a smaller number of viable candidates. With these firms, you might be asked to do a lengthy telephone or online video interview with the consultant or respond in writing to a list of specific questions. You have to decide if this is an investment of time you want to make in order to be considered for this particular position.

Disclosing Personal Information

Senior positions are often very public, and the committee will be thinking about more than just your credentials. Particularly when applying for a presidency, you should expect that there will be interest in your personal life. It may not be fair, but it is a reality.

In making an application, you have to think about whether and how much to disclose about your personal life at the start of the process. One set of issues has to do with your family situation. Straight cis men often make a reference to their wife and children at the end of their letters. It humanizes them and indicates that there is familial support for any needed relocation. And, of course, it establishes them as a safe candidate. As a woman, you have a more difficult set of choices to make.

I have always opted to disclose potentially disqualifying information in the initial letter. Knowing that some institutions do not hire Jewish leaders, I find a way to work in this aspect of my identity in my cover letter (e.g., "Memphis is especially attractive to us because of its lively Jewish community," or "I would look forward to learning more about the college's Hillel and Jewish life programming"). My thinking is that if this is going to be an issue for the search committee, I would rather know at the outset and avoid wasting my time in an application process that isn't going to go anywhere. Similarly, a sign-off that says "My partner, Susan, is enthusiastic about this application" would weed out institutions where sexual orientation is an issue. It is also fine to say, "I recognize that I would be the first Black woman [or woman with a disability, and so on] to hold this position, and I look forward to thinking about ways that we could work together to make this a celebratory moment for the college."

It is also standard practice for colleges to do a credit check before hiring senior leaders. Having your financial house in order helps make the case that you will be a wise steward of institutional resources. If there are likely to be anomalies in your credit report, it is important for you to have an explanation and to consider disclosing that ahead of time.

Ultimately, there is no right or wrong answer to the question of whether to disclose personal information up front. You have to decide based on what feels right to you.

References

You are likely to be asked for a list of references early in the process, but no one will contact them until you are a finalist and only after you give your express permission. On the initial list, I recommend putting only people you are absolutely comfortable telling about your application. Even if they won't get called unless you are a finalist, you should never include someone as a reference without both their permission and their agreement that they will give you a positive recommendation. If you advance in the search, you will at some point have to tell your current supervisor that you are a candidate since the president or board chair will want to speak to them directly. My advice is to wait until this is necessary.

For your other references, choose people who can speak positively about you and your work from a variety of perspectives. Your list might include a peer, someone who supervised you, someone whom you supervised, and a mentee. Make sure you provide them with the job description, your CV, and your cover letter. Consider as well whether they are likely to come across as enthusiastic. Some people are so flat that they make terrible references even if the content of what they say is very positive.

Interviewing Effectively

After you have submitted your materials, you will probably get a call fairly quickly from the search consultant, letting you know whether you have advanced to the next step. This is likely to be an off-campus interview at a hotel near an airport. If you hear nothing for more than a month or so, you can assume you are not being advanced, but you should call the search consultant to confirm. Sometimes, search committees move slowly.

You will be flown in and likely housed at the same hotel where the interview takes place. Search committees may meet with up to ten candidates over a two-day period, so efforts will be made to keep you from running into other candidates. You may be asked to lay low, order room service, and otherwise protect your privacy and the privacy of the other applicants.

Some consultants like to divide the committee into two groups, each of which meets with the candidate for forty-five minutes at a time. Others like to have the whole committee meet with the candidate for an hour or so. Make sure you understand ahead of time what will happen so you can manage your energy effectively.

As you prepare, remember that the committee will be asking roughly the same questions of each candidate, so the questions will likely be pretty generic ("Tell us about your experience as a fund-raiser") rather than specifically about you ("Tell us about the gift you received to fund the new major in neuroscience"). It is up to you to personalize your answers.

Assume that the questions will generally match the things that are mentioned in the prospectus as key areas of focus. If you haven't been on an interview in a while, practice answering some imaginary questions and timing yourself. If the interview is seventy-five minutes, and they want to leave ten minutes for you to ask questions, and they have eight questions, you can figure out about how long you should take to answer each one. Think about one or two accomplishments or brief stories to go with every key item.

When I interview, I try to begin each answer with a sentence that describes generally how I think about the topic at hand ("Successful fund-raising requires a combination of good metrics, compelling vision, and deep relationships") and then give an example or tell a story that illustrates this. I also tie in my answer to the issues facing that college—showing I have done my homework and understand who they are. The general sentence conveys a sense of competence and thoughtfulness. I am showing that my actions are grounded in a broader set of leadership abilities and experiences. The specific examples show that I can answer the question more directly and that I have lots of accomplishments on which to draw. And tying what I said to their campus helps them start to imagine me in their world.

Your answers should be mostly forward-looking even as you cite past accomplishments and experiences. You aren't applying for an award. You are applying for a job. This means that your reply should be less about the details of what you have done in the past and more about the way these past experiences have prepared you to tackle the challenges of this institution's future.

I also plan a list of questions to ask. My goal is to get them talking about things they care about and to learn how they think. A question about a recent big decision is a good one. So is a question about what should *never* change at their institution. The more you can turn this part of the interview into a conversation, the more likely it is that the search committee members can imagine you as part of their team.

Be yourself, and be as relaxed as you can be in the circumstances. I believe strongly in the motto that while they will forget what you said, they will never forget how you made them feel. Do everything you can to make them feel engaged and excited to continue the conversation with you.

My husband is a professional performer, and one lesson I have learned from him is that everything on stage has a meaning. The interview starts as soon as you enter the room and doesn't end until you leave it. The committee members will be watching how you make an entrance and how you greet people. Especially in an interview for a presidency, they will be looking for executive presence—a sense that you can command a room. I once read a definition of charisma that said it was presence plus power plus warmth.[1] Keep that equation in mind as you imagine how you will walk in, shake hands with each member of the group, and sit down at the table. Aim to make eye contact with everyone there at least once during the interview.

Wear something that makes you feel strong and isn't fussy. A suit is great but not if you will be tugging at your skirt or tucking in your blouse when you stand up. The male candidates will all be in dark suits. You have an opportunity to stand out a bit with your style. I opt for a neutral dress, a jacket, a stylish pair of shoes, and a sleek handbag or briefcase: simple but sophisticated. I avoid bare legs, shoes that are hard to walk in, and anything too trendy. I am helping them imagine what a woman president looks like.

Waiting is often the hardest part of the search process. Once you have completed the airport interview, you may be excited and hopeful. It will be hard to be patient and wait to learn whether you will advance. My advice is to distract yourself—and promise yourself a treat if you hear negative news. Resist telling many people about the interview, and don't start packing or envisioning the decoration for your new office. You still have a road ahead.

Becoming a Finalist

When the search consultant calls to say that the committee loved your initial interview and has invited you to participate in the next round, let yourself enjoy this sense of accomplishment. This is a big deal. You are a finalist or a near-finalist. At this point, they have narrowed their pool down to a group that is likely no bigger than four. You are being seriously considered for this senior-level job.

This is also when you have to decide if you are serious too. If you agree to be a finalist, you should be pretty sure you would take the job if it is offered. Of course, there might be something that you discover during the next round of interviews that turns you off. But moving forward at this point is an indication of your serious interest and excitement.

If you have a major personal reservation—about the location, for example—this is the time to do the soul searching to decide if you can live with it or live with it under certain conditions. If your partner isn't already completely onboard, this is the time to have the heart-to-heart conversation about whether they are ready to move with you. If there are deal-breaker items, reiterate those to the search consultant. If they can't be met, then you should not go forward.

There is a lot of variability in the ways a second-round interview can be structured. The search is down to a small number of candidates, and the search committee is looking to get to know each of them better. How this part of the search is handled will tell you a lot about the college and its priorities. Aim to get as much information as possible from the search consultant about what to expect. Good questions include: With whom will I be meeting? How long will the meetings be? Am I expected to make a presentation of any sort? Will there be social events, such as a dinner? Is my partner expected to join me?

You can also ask for additional information from the college. It is common that a budget overview is sent to you at this point as well as other insider information that can help you prepare for the interview. If there is something specific you want to see or know, ask for it. Obviously, all of this information is given to you in trust, and you should keep it completely confidential whether or not you get the job.

At this point, it is likely that you will be asked to meet with people beyond the search committee. When I interviewed for the provost position at Muhlenberg College, I met with the department chairs, the vice presidents, and a small group of student leaders. The process at Austin College was similar but also included leaders of the staff council. At Rhodes, the process was more confidential (I was a sitting president by then) and included three representatives from the faculty, three student leaders, and several emeriti trustees.

If this is a vice presidential or dean search, you will likely spend time alone with the president. This may be over a meal or at her home. She is assessing the quality of the potential relationship she can build with you. She wants to understand how you solve problems and what you can bring to her team. She is also looking for signs that you are hardworking, enthusiastic, and loyal.

You are looking to assess many of the same things about her. Is this someone you can stand behind and with whom you want to spend time? Will she be a supportive boss? Can she build a team? Is her vision for the college one that you can support? If you can't picture this kind of relationship with the president, then this job may not be for you even if you like all the other things about it.

You are also likely to be asked to give some kind of presentation. This may be a ten-minute review of your vision for the college at the start of a meeting with the search committee or a full-blown lecture for the entire campus followed by a question-and-answer period. Make sure you understand exactly what is expected so you are properly prepare to shine.

This second round of interviewing is likely to be intense and tightly packed. You need to pace yourself. Bring a snack of some kind because you may spend meals responding to questions and won't have much time to actually eat. You may be expected to tromp around campus, so choose your shoes accordingly. It is unlikely that the search coordinators are thinking about the challenges women face in choosing appropriate footwear, so be prepared for a variety of possibilities. It is fine to wear your heels for the meetings and change into stylish flats for the campus tour.

You should expect that some questions will stem from worries that as a woman you might not be up to the job. I was once asked in an interview if I liked football. I have sometimes had to specifically emphasize my business acumen and my ability to make tough decisions, qualities not always associated with women in the minds of some search committee members.

By the time you reach the second interview, the committee has already determined that you are qualified for the position. The issue now is all about the abstract concept of fit. Do your strengths match up with the priorities set for the position? Is the timing right for the kind of leadership you will provide? Do you bring personal characteristics that will engage important constituencies? Will you be happy in this work and at this school? Do you like the people with whom you would be working? Do they like you?

Fit has often been used as a way to exclude women and people of color. If fit is defined as a match with the institution's current identity—as similarity to those already in the room—or as someone who won't make anyone feel uncomfortable, it is likely to count against you if you are breaking down barriers. But fit is also about a match between the institution's aspirational identity and the new leader. You can enhance the committee's ability to see you as a good fit by identifying with the college's history *and* its future and showing them that hiring you is an evolutionary next step in the institution's expanding access.

Because women are still underrepresented at this level of leadership, even straight cis white women count as a "diversity" hire at many institutions. For queer women and women of color, the "diversity" label is even more likely. There has probably already been discussion about whether the institution is ready for you. You can assume that the committee has received comments about you that depend on or reinforce gender and racial stereotypes. Your looks, wardrobe, commitment to smiling, and ability to project both the feminine ideal of warmth and the (masculine) presidential ideal of command will be evaluated. In a perfect world, the search committee has received some guidance from the search consultant about how to parse these issues. But this is not something on which you can count.

On the other hand, there will likely be many people who are energized and excited by your candidacy. They may see you as a symbol of institutional progress and as a role model for others. When I was hired at Rhodes College, some of the women alumni referenced the college's famous Gothic architecture and announced my hiring as the first woman president with the hashtag #BreakingtheStainedGlassCeiling. At each of my institutions, the Jewish alumni reached out to me with pride and enthusiasm. Many search committees will be delighted that the best man for the job turned out to be a woman.

In some searches, there may be a third round of interviews or a conversation with the president or board chair just prior to a decision being made. The purpose is to answer any lingering questions and to gauge your enthusiasm for the position. This is when you should consider taking the risk of affirming your commitment. When I interviewed at Rhodes, this was the moment I said to the committee, "If you offer me the job, I will accept it." No committee wants to have an offer rejected. Your genuine enthusiasm will be appreciated.

The End of the Search

You can drop out of a search at any point, but it is best to do so as soon as you realize that you would not take the job if it were offered. This might happen after the first interview. Sometimes, you just get a bad vibe from the committee. Or you might suddenly get cold feet about leaving your current position. Take those feelings seriously.

At the second interview, something might become apparent that really turns you off. It is perfectly appropriate to let the search consultant know that you cannot continue in the process. She would rather know this now than to be faced with your turning down an actual offer. And she just might have a perspective that could change your mind. She has gotten to know the institution and may have additional information that you had not considered.

At any point in this process, you may learn that the committee has decided you will not be advancing in the search. This always feels lousy—even if you are ambivalent about the job. In order to do well in the search process, you have had to picture yourself in this new role. You have had to fall a little bit in love with the new institution. Being turned down brings on feelings of rejection and disappointment. You have a bit of a broken heart.

Let yourself feel disappointed. Buy that consolation prize you promised yourself, and ask for support from the people who love you best. Do all the things that helped you get over a crush in the past—a new haircut, a brighter lipstick, eating ice cream out of the container, looking at other options, whatever works for you.

Do not, however, let this rejection discourage you from trying again. It is easy to think that everyone lands a great job on their first try—because the successes are the only ones talked about. But this just isn't true. Almost no one gets a big job on their first try, and many people go through multiple interviews before landing a position. In some ways, it is not even about you—it is about the chemistry and the match. Giving up ensures that you will never succeed. It may seem like cold comfort, but not getting a job is often a blessing. If they don't want you, it is likely that the job would have made you unhappy. You will eventually look back on this moment with a sense of relief.

Learn as much as you can from this experience. The search consultant can be a great source of feedback about what worked or didn't work in your application and interview. Then, dry your tears and try again until you have found the perfect match.

Responding to an Offer

It is a wonderful feeling to hear that you are the successful candidate. Take a moment to feel very proud of yourself and to celebrate. This is a major accomplishment.

Sometimes, the search consultant calls you to confirm that you will say yes, and then the board chair or president phones you to actually offer the job. When I have gotten this kind of call, I have expressed my appreciation and enthusiasm. You won't want to spend too much time talking because you will be dying to get off the phone and let your family know.

This initial call does not typically include a discussion of the details of the contract. You will usually be told that a written offer will be sent for you to review. It is good to indicate that you look forward to finalizing things and that you don't anticipate that the contract discussion will be prolonged or difficult.

The written offer should include salary and benefit information as well as any special details (tenure, a car allowance, sabbatical eligibility, and so on). Presidential contracts are more complicated, and I advise you to have an attorney represent you. This is for your protection and also so that you have someone to do the "dirty work" if there are issues that need to be negotiated. Your attorney can mark up the document and send it to the college's attorney.

Some public universities engage in the presidential contract negotiations prior to offering the job. They want to make agreements with each of the finalists so that the successful candidate can be announced as soon as the board votes. Private institutions expect that there will be a confidential negotiation process between the time of the offer and the announcement.

When a salary figure is offered, you should always ask what factors were used in arriving at it. The answer is usually a combination of facts about the salary structure at the institution and facts about you—your credentials, length of experience, and so on. You want to understand this so that you can clear up any misunderstandings (e.g., "Actually, I have been an associate dean for six years, not five") and so that you can respond to the salary offer in a realistic way. In my experience, women are less likely to negotiate than men, but when they do they are often more successful because they are thoughtful and realistic in how they approach the negotiation process.

The more you understand about the overall financial structure and the compensation scale at an institution, the better you will be able to shape your requests. Public institutions are more likely to have firm guidelines in place, and since all salaries are public information, you can easily see where the offered salary lands you. Private institutions have to report the salaries of their most senior executives on their 990 disclosure forms.[2] Some administrative salaries are also published in the *Chronicle of Higher Education*. Be aware that most of these public sources are out of date by a year or two.

Resist the request to name a salary figure. The onus should be on the hiring manager to make a fair offer. If you are pressed, you can say something such as "I expect to be compensated fairly," or "I expect that my salary will reflect the nature of the job." Unless you think the salary conversation is really going to be a deal-breaker, I recommend adopting a collaborative tone—assuring the hiring manager that you want the job and that you will work with them to find a compensation package that is fair to the institution and fair to you. It is always appropriate to ask what the previous holder of the position was paid and to say that you would like to earn at least that much.

Once an offer is made, it is also appropriate to ask how that figure compares with the salaries of others in similar roles (e.g., "Will this salary place me in the top or bottom half of deans at the university?").

You can also explicitly ask whether your salary would be comparable to men in similar roles—or to white people in similar roles if you are a person of color. If the hiring manager is unable or unwilling to answer questions about equity, that should be concerning to you and might tell you something about the climate of that institution.

You should also ask about the college's history with salary increases and what you can expect annually. Politically, it is easier to ask for and to receive a higher starting salary than it is to ask for or receive larger annual raises. Therefore, take the initial offer very seriously. It is especially important to have a frank conversation about salary if you are being promoted from within. This is a situation where it can be easy to be offered (and to accept) less than what would be offered to an outside candidate. You should explicitly discuss this with the hiring manager.

Once you have gotten answers to your questions, you should either graciously accept the offered salary ("I appreciate your efforts to be fair") or name a reasonable counterfigure. You could also suggest other forms of compensation that could make this a more attractive position for you. Again, the more you understand about the institution, the more likely you are to make a reasonable request

Be aware that hiring managers get frustrated if you engage in these conversations in a way that seems unreasonable or hostile. And stressing how fabulous you are is not the way forward either. Focus instead on how the compensation will help you do your job better (e.g., "A budget for conference travel will keep me engaged in the national conversation"). Unless you are truly ready to walk away, do not couch your requests as demands. That approach can result in the job offer itself being rescinded.

You may choose to accept a parallel salary or even a reduction in salary. One path toward senior-level leadership is to move from a larger institution to a smaller one or from a wealthier institution to a poorer one. You will be trading up in terms of job title, experience, and opportunity, but you may be moving into a less robust pay structure. Do your homework ahead of time so that you are not applying for jobs that won't pay what you need. Think, too, about the added expenses of your new position: a new wardrobe or higher dry-cleaning bills, extended childcare hours, a longer commute, and so on.

Perks and benefits vary by institution and by role. Provosts and academic deans should expect tenure, for example, and presidents should expect support for entertaining in their home and for dues in organizations that will assist with fund-raising. In each case, think ahead of time about what really matters to you. The fewer things you ask for, the more likely you are to receive them. Would you consider trading tenure for a higher salary? Is having a car or a phone paid for by the institution more important to you than additional salary?

When all the negotiations are completed, be gracious and excited as you accept the offer. This is the start of a long-term relationship. You want to get off on a strong footing.

You also need to think about how you will announce this news. Your first call should be to your current supervisor. The broader announcement needs to be a collaboration between your current institution and your new one. The new one will likely want to make a splash about your hiring, and your current institution will want to make the announcement in a way that is reassuring to the campus and indicates the path to finding your replacement.

You do not want to get ahead of their process. But you also want to be able to tell close colleagues before they see the press release. This is a tricky balance. Ideally, you can get permission to make some confidential calls the evening before the public announcement. Keep your list narrow, and emphasize that this is embargoed news.

Enjoy the excitement of this time. And then prepare for the next set of transitions.

Moving Forward in Your Career

Most of us find that our careers advance through a combination of strategy and luck. Understanding the search process is important so that you can be fully prepared to compete for a job when it is advertised. But fortunate timing and happenstance matter as well. Most successful women can identify opportunities that they learned about through an offhand comment from a colleague or through a seemingly random professional connection. This is one reward for being in the right place at the right time.

Similarly, most successful women can point to opportunities they missed out on through poor timing or bad luck. I know one woman whose daughter was hospitalized with a serious illness the day before her final interview for a presidency. Another friend got food poisoning on the way to her airport interview and had to struggle through it looking green and weak.

Neither of these women were able to perform at their best, and neither got the job. But they both forged ahead and were able to successfully change positions the following year.

Preparing to take advantage of good luck and being able to rebound from bad luck are both important. So is a willingness to take risks. Stepping into an interim role is a prelude to permanent career advancement for many women. It takes courage to suddenly take on new responsibilities, but interim service offers a chance to learn a great deal and to add an important credential to your CV.

Understanding the search process allows you to prepare as much as possible so that you can take calculated risks and make the most of the lucky breaks that come your way.

Putting It into Practice

Entering a search requires dedicated time and energy as well as the ability to tolerate the stress of being judged. It is not something to begin lightly. Search consultants can be a great source of advice about your readiness for a position and the kinds of skills you might need to develop to move ahead. Thinking bravely and clearly about where you are in your career and where you want to go will help you focus on winning the right kind of job.

REFLECTION QUESTIONS

Which job ads intrigue me?

What seems exciting about those positions?

What have I accomplished in my present position?

Where would I be willing to live?

Have I discussed the possibility of a move with my family?

Am I prepared to market myself?

Am I ready to have a conversation with a search consultant?

Am I ready to leap should a lucky break come my way?

Concluding Thoughts

———

LEADERSHIP IS an incredible privilege. It offers the opportunity and the responsibility to make meaningful, lasting change in your institution and therefore for generations of students. Rising to the challenges of leadership transforms us professionally and personally. As you reflect on the conceptual tools and advice I have shared in this book, I hope you are filled with enthusiasm for the road ahead. It is not an easy path, but it is deeply fulfilling.

In this book I have suggested that you give thought to the way your professional identity changes as you become a leader, to managing the complexity of power and conflict, and to finding joy in your work. You have been shown a model for understanding the three pillars of your institution and for developing a vision to align them. I hope you are working on the skills you'll need to assume a senior position and are prepared to engage successfully in the search process. These tools have helped me, and they will serve you well now and on your future career path.

I consider each of you to be part of my network, and I look forward to hearing about your progress and the ways you are transforming your institution. You can subscribe to my newsletter at www.MarjorieHass

.com. Every month, I share my latest insights about creative leadership, and I help women leaders to connect with each other in an ongoing way.

My primary goal in writing this book was to offer support and advice gleaned from my personal experiences and from the experiences of other women. I hope I have sufficiently emphasized these three core ideas:

- Lead with your mind, body, and spirit. Leadership requires your best thinking, but it is not only a "head" activity. It calls on every part of you, and the more deeply you embrace the holistic nature of this work, the more effective you are. Understanding your own soul and the soul of your institution allows you to unleash your gifts in ways that make meaningful, positive change.
- Find ways to support your own growth and happiness. Burnout is a distinct possibility when the work you do is inherently difficult. Develop ways to nurture your creativity, celebrate the small wins, and build a network. These form the foundation that will enable you to flourish over time. Avoiding burnout is particularly important for women who engage in a great deal of emotional and other forms of labor at home and in their communities.
- Leave the door open wider behind you. You don't need to wait until you have completed your career to make opportunities for others. From wherever you are now, you can be a sponsor or a mentor. By making this type of support an explicit part of your career goals, you will participate in the wider work of diversifying leadership at all levels. Every time you take a step forward, look to see whom you can bring with you. Once you are settled in, turn back and help someone else take their next step.

One of my deepest beliefs is that self-knowledge and self-development are essential if one is to lead effectively. The visibility of leadership roles and the power they confer demand humility and internal reflection. Otherwise, the work is merely self-serving. At the same time, good leaders have to become experts at renewal and self-care. Learning to walk this fine line is an ongoing task, but it will help you to sustain your work over time.

I am writing this conclusion in the midst of one of the most disruptive and challenging periods I have faced as a leader. Responding to COVID-19 has demanded every ounce of skill I possess, as well as the skill of every member of our campus. Over the past few months, I have cried more, laughed more, worried more, and found greater reasons for hope than ever before. Higher education is likely to be reeling from this pandemic for some time. Our sector will survive, but if it is to do more than that—if it is to rise and thrive—it will need visionary leadership. Preparing talented women to lead in this environment thus feels especially urgent.

I hope you feel called to this work, and I am grateful to be able to assist you along the way. Remember: the unique experiences and perspectives you bring to your activities as a creative leader will deeply enrich the institution you serve. Let your light shine.

NOTES

Introduction

1. Yoni Blumberg, "Companies with More Female Executives Make More Money—Here's Why," CNBC, March 2, 2018, https://www.cnbc.com/2018/03/02/why-companies-with-female-managers-make-more-money.html.

2. Kweilin Ellingrud, "How Women Leaders Change Company Dynamics," *Forbes*, January 30, 2019, www.forbes.com/sites/kweilinellingrud/2019/01/30/how-women-leaders-change-company-dynamics/#6d20c4447335.

Chapter 1. Transforming Your Professional Identity

1. William Bridges, *The Way of Transition: Embracing Life's Most Difficult Moments* (Hachette Books, 2001).

2. Susan Resneck Pierce, *On Being Presidential: A Guide for College and University Leaders* (Wiley and Sons, 2012).

Chapter 2. Navigating Power and Conflict

1. Quoted in Karen A. Longman and Susan R. Madsen, eds., *Women and Leadership in Higher Education* (Information Age Publishing, 2014), 180.

2. Mimi Wolverton, Beverly L. Bower, and Adrienne E. Hyle, *Women at the Top: What Women University and College Presidents Say about Effective Leadership* (Stylus, 2009), 118.

3. "Take the Thomas-Kilmann Conflict Mode Instrument (TKI)," https://kilmanndiagnostics.com/overview-thomas-kilmann-conflict-mode-instrument-tki/.

4. Brian Emerson and Kelly Lewis, *Navigating Polarities: Using Polarity Thinking to Lead Transformation* (Paradox Press, 2019).

Chapter 3. Finding Joy in Your Work

1. Marcus Aurelius, *Meditations*, translated by Gregory Hays (Modern Library, 2002), 33.

2. For example, see Brené Brown, *Daring Greatly* (Penguin Random House, 2012). A deeper analysis of how shame operates and intrudes on creativity can be found in the work of Jungian analyst and art therapist Vibeke Skov. See her *Shame and Creativity: From Affect towards Individuation* (Routledge, 2018).

Chapter 4. Growing as a Leader

1. Aristotle, *Nicomachean Ethics*, translated by David Ross (Oxford University Press, 2009).

2. Jack Zenger and Joseph Folkman, "Research: Women Score Higher than Men in Most Leadership Skills," *Harvard Business Review*, June 25, 2019, https://hbr.org/2019/06/research-women-score-higher-than-men-in-most-leadership-skills.

3. Lee Gardner, "What Happens When Women Run Colleges?," *Chronicle of Higher Education*, June 30, 2019, https://www.chronicle.com/interactives/20190630-womenincharge.

4. Jeffrey L. Buller, *Positive Academic Leadership: How to Stop Putting Out Fires and Start Making a Difference* (Wiley and Sons, 2013).

5. John P. Kotter, *Leading Change* (Harvard Business Review Press, 2012).

6. The term "decision fatigue" was coined by psychologist Roy F. Baumeister to describe his finding that the quality of decisions goes down in relation to the number of decisions that have been made, irrespective of the importance or challenge of those previous decisions. See, for example, Baumeister, "Ego Depletion and Self-Control Failure: An Energy Model of the Self's Executive Function," *Self and Identity* 1(2) (2002): 129–136.

7. Sun Tzu, *The Art of War*, translated by James Trapp (Amber Books, 2011), sec. 8, 12.

8. Joanna Barsh and Susie Cranston, *How Remarkable Women Lead* (Crown Business, 2009). See also Joanna Barsh and Johanne Lavoie, *Centered Leadership* (Currency, 2014).

Chapter 5. Crafting a Vision

1. Steven Pressfield, *The Artist's Journey: The Wake of the Hero's Journey and the Lifelong Pursuit of Meaning* (Black Irish Entertainment, 2019), 23.

2. You can learn about Parker's work at www.thecreationgame.com.

3. Carolyn R. Hodges and Olga M. Welch, *Truth without Tears: African American Women Deans Share Lessons in Leadership* (Harvard Education Press, 2018), 62.

4. A good overview of strategic planning can be found in *On Strategy* (Harvard Business School Publishing, 2011).

Chapter 6. Building Your Skills

1. *The Successful President of Tomorrow: The 5 Skills Future Leaders Will Need* (Chronicle of Higher Education, 2019), https://store.chronicle.com/products/the-successful-president-of-tomorrow-the-5-skills-future-leaders-need.

Chapter 7. Winning the Job

1. Olivia Fox Cabane, *The Charisma Myth: How Anyone Can Master the Art and Science of Personal Magnetism* (Portfolio, 2012).

2. You can find the 990 forms for all nonprofit entities at guidestar.org.

INDEX

absorbing energetic state, 61, 65
accommodators model of conflict, 44
administration: and first jump, 16; vs. leadership, 8–9; skills, 3
advisors, career, 10, 111
Agnes Scott College, 73–74
airport interviews, 123, 131
ambition, 5, 7, 18, 20–21, 127
American Conference of Academic Deans, 28–29
American Council on Education, 29
anger, 41, 43, 47–49, 52, 58–59
anxiety, 17, 24–25, 58, 59
appearance: comments on, 36–37; and interviews, 133, 135, 136; and photographs, 31; and presidency, 29, 31; transitions in, 19, 25–27, 29. *See also* clothes
The Artist's Journey (Pressfield), 90
The Art of War (Sun Tzu), 85–86
assessment. *See* self-examination
Association of American Colleges and Universities, 29
athletic directors, 16, 19
Austin College, 5, 76, 94, 119, 134
authority: and conflict styles, 45, 49; and covert disrespect, 50–52; undermining of, 45. *See also* power; responsibility
autonomy, 18, 19–20, 86
avoiders model of conflict, 44, 45

back of house, transition to, 19, 27
bad news, communicating, 41–43
Barsh, Joanna, 85–86, 88
Baumeister, Roy F., 148n6
"beginner's mind" insights, 18, 97–98
benefits, in offer, 138, 141
benevolence, as virtue, 85, 86

board of trustees: and appearance, 26; and budget responsibility, 106; and disruptors, 80; and hiring decisions, 121, 136–37; and internal candidate support, 126; involvement in mission, business model, and culture, 77; reporting to, 19, 29; and vision, 98
boss: being a, 19, 23, 110–11; having a, 19, 22
boundaries, managing, 23, 39–40, 43
Bower, Beverly L., 39
breadwinner, transition to, 19, 24–25
Bridges, William, 17
Brown, Brené, 60
Bucklin, Mary L., 37
budget officers, working with, 107–8
budgets and budgeting skills, 38–39, 106–8, 112–13, 134
Buller, Jeffrey, 71
burnout, 25, 60, 65, 145
business model: and decision-making, 82; and identifying needed changes, 75–77, 88, 113–14; slides on, 98; and vision development, 90–91, 96, 97, 98, 104

calm, 43, 45, 47, 49
candidates, internal, 124–27, 140
chairs, department, 16, 22, 106
change: communications on, 77, 78–79; creating, 77–79; disruptors, 79–80; identifying, 74–77, 88, 113–14; questions on, 88; resistance, 100; and role of leadership, 12, 71–73, 88; stages of, 77–79; vs. transitions, 17. *See also* vision
chaplains, 43, 122
charisma, 95, 132
clothes, 19, 25–27, 29, 81, 133, 135, 136
coaches, executive, 30

collaborators model of conflict, 44
communication: of bad news, 41–43; on change, 77, 78–79; clarity in, 40–43; on decision-making, 9; and inclusive language, 79; media skills, 30, 31; and presidency, 30–31, 113; social media, 57; with storytelling, 100, 104, 131; and strategic planning, 101–2; transparency in, 57; and vision, 98–100
communications directors, 31
community relations, 30–31, 73
community relations experts, 31
competition and personal criticism, 57
competitors model of conflict, 44, 45
compliments and covert disrespect, 51
compromisers model of conflict, 44
confidence, 5, 20, 21, 68, 79–80
confidentiality, 27, 122, 127, 134, 139, 141
conflicts, 12, 43–46, 47–50, 52
connecting, as capability, 85, 86
contract negotiations, 138–41
conversation, 38–39, 61, 71, 94, 132, 136–37
Council of Independent Colleges, 29
courage, as virtue, 85, 86
Courtice, Tom, 8, 119
cover letters, 127–28, 130
covert disrespect, 50–52
COVID-19 pandemic, 13, 146
creativity, 12, 96–98, 104, 145
credit checks, 129–30
crises, 113, 114, 124
criticism, personal, 54, 55, 56–57, 65
crying and tears, 49–50
culture: and appearance, 26–27; and changes, 75–77, 78, 88; and decision-making, 82; and inclusive language, 79; and searches, 121–22; and vision, 91, 96, 97, 98, 104
curriculum vitae (CV), 127–28, 130

daughter paradigm, 51–52
daydreams and creating vision, 94
deal-breaker requests, 123–24, 134
deans: author as, 4; as first jump role, 16; organizations for, 28–29; role of, 71, 72, 87, 108, 112
decision fatigue, 81
decision-making: and budget responsibility, 107; communicating process, 9; and

dissent, 20; in searches, 121, 126, 136–37; and strategic thinking, 101, 102–3; strategies for, 80–82; transitions in, 21–22; and vision, 82, 90
defensive thinking, 59
deflecting energetic state, 61, 65
department chairs, 16, 22, 106
development officers, 111–12
discipline, as virtue, 85
disrespect, covert, 50–52
disruptors, 79–80
diversity: and author, 2, 6; and inclusive language, 79; and mission reframing, 76; and vision, 99. *See also* first, being; queer women; women of color
donors, 36, 111–12
dreams, 17, 94

emotions. *See* feelings
employees: privacy of, 83; transition to being, 19, 22–23; transition to having, 19, 23, 41–43, 106, 110–11. *See also* firing; hiring
empowering actions, 77
energy and energy management, 60–62, 65, 85, 86, 131, 135
engagement, 85, 86, 94, 95, 98–100, 101–2, 103, 104
environmental scan, 101
evaluations, personnel, 41–43, 110–11
executive coaches, 30
expertise, 18, 21–22, 115

faculty: and academic leadership, 70, 86–87; budget responsibility, 106–7; faculty identity, 86; and leadership virtues, 86–87; mission, business model, and culture involvement, 76–77; on search committees, 122; transitions of, 3, 16–17, 18–23, 110–11; and vision, 90, 91
family and spouses: comments on status, 36; effect on, 4–5, 16, 32; expectations for women, 6, 62; and salary, 25; and searches, 129; and work-life alignment, 62–64
Family Educational Rights and Privacy Act, 83
fear, 59
feedback, 23, 27, 110, 116, 138

feelings: and bad news, 43; in conflicts, 12, 47–50, 51, 52; and rejection, 20–21, 127, 137–38; and salary, 24–25; stress as catchall for, 58–59, 65; and transitions, 16–18; and vision, 94. *See also* anger; happiness

firing, 23, 41–43, 110–11

first, being: addressing early, 129; author as, 5–6, 122–23, 129, 136; and fit, 135–36; and peer group, 28–29; questions on, 122–23

fit concept, in job searches, 135–36

forecasting revenues, 108–9

framing, as capability/virtue, 85, 86

friends, 4–5, 16, 19, 23, 28–29, 30, 39–40, 43

front of house, transition from, 19, 27

fund-raising skills, 106, 111–13

future memory, 94

Gardner, Lee, 68, 69

generality, transition to, 18, 21–22, 29

goals vs. vision, 92–93, 101

governance, academic, 70, 90

guiding coalition, 77

guilt, 24–25, 62–63

hair and makeup. *See* appearance

happiness: barriers to, 56–60; celebrating successes, 53–54, 72, 145; and energy management, 60–62, 65; importance of, 12, 64–65, 145; and integrity, 55–56, 57, 65; lists, 56, 65; questions on, 65; and secrecy, 55, 65, 83; and virtues, 84; work-life alignment, 62–64

Helm, Randy, 4, 8, 114–15

hiring responsibility and skills, 19, 23, 106, 110–11, 112–13, 114–15. *See also* searches, job

Hodges, Carolyn R., 99

hosting duties, 32, 141

human resources, 42, 43, 110

Hyle, Adrienne E., 39

identity: as concern for women, 5, 11–12; and expertise, 21–22; faculty identity, 86; group identity, 19, 28–29; questions for, 4, 15, 20–27, 29–32; and virtues, 84. *See also* identity, transitions in

identity, transitions in: vs. changes, 17; from faculty positions, 3, 16–17, 18–23, 110–11; general, 18, 19, 23–29; and jump concept, 15–19; list of, 18–19; overview of, 14–16; and peer group, 4–5, 16, 19, 28–29, 30, 40; and presidency, 18, 19, 29–32; questions on, 4, 15, 20–27, 29–32; and self-examination, 17–19, 32–33

impostor syndrome, 17, 59

inclusive language, 79

individual, transition from, 19, 23–24, 30

information: and decision-making, 82; and job searches, 118, 119, 120, 124, 129–30, 134, 138, 142; personal, 129–30

integrating energetic state, 61, 65

integrity and happiness, 55–56, 57, 65

interim positions, 124, 125–26, 142

internal candidates, 124–27, 140

interviews: clothes for, 133, 135, 136; feedback on, 138; first-round/airport, 123, 131; preliminary phone, 129; questions for, 131–32, 134, 135; second-round, 123, 134–36; strategies for, 130–33; third-round, 136–37

Jewish, being first president, 5–6, 122–23, 129, 136

job searches. *See* searches, job

joy. *See* happiness

jump concept, 15–19

Kiss, Elizabeth, 73–74

Kotter, John P., 77–78

leadership: assessing readiness, 7; complexity of academic, 69–71, 86–87; defining, 71–73; as fulfilling, 144; lack of models for, 12, 67–68; vs. management/administration, 8–9, 72; motivations for, 14–15; positive effects of female, 2, 6–7; as practice or journey, 9–10, 67, 71–72, 74, 88, 145; as relational, 73, 86; resources on, 70, 71; traits, 3, 6, 68–69, 118; virtues of, 83–87, 88. *See also* change; decision-making; happiness; identity, transitions in; power; skills; symbols; vision

Leading Change (Kotter), 77–78

legal issues, 42, 83, 138

letting go in transitions, 17–18
lifestyle, 19, 31–32, 62–64
liminal period, 17–18, 74
loss, feelings of, 17
loyalty, 22, 115–16, 134

"Madame President" (Bucklin), 37
makeup and hair. *See* appearance
management: conflict, 43–46, 52; energy, 60–62, 65, 85, 86, 131, 135; vs. leadership, 72; personnel skills, 106, 110–11, 112–13; time, 20, 24, 31–32, 96–97
Marcus Aurelius, 54–55, 65, 82
maybe, saying, 41
meaning, as capability/virtue, 85
media skills and training, 30, 31, 57
Meditations (Marcus Aurelius), 54–55
memory, future, 94
men: anger from, 47; appearance of, 25–26, 81; family/identity concerns, 5; lessons for, 2; and salary negotiations, 139, 140; statistics on, 5–6
mentoring, 1, 10–11, 145
mission: and changes, 75–77, 113–14; and decision-making, 82; vs. profit, 69; reframing examples, 73–74, 76; and strategic planning, 101; as term, 102; and vision, 90–91, 96, 97, 98, 104
money: budget responsibility, 106–8, 112–13; credit checks, 129–30; fundraising, 106, 111–13; revenue responsibility, 106, 108–9, 112–13. *See also* salary
Moreland, Milton, 73
mother paradigm, 51–52
Muhlenberg College, 3–5, 7–8, 38–39, 76, 119, 134

negotiations, contract, 138–41
no, saying, 41
nominations, 125, 127
notes, 18, 97–98

Obama, Barack, 81
offers, responding to, 138–41
On Being Presidential (Pierce), 29

Parker, George, 94
peer groups, 4–5, 16, 19, 28–29, 30, 40
perks, in offer, 64, 141

personnel responsibility skills, 106, 110–11, 112–13, 114–16
photographs, 31
Pierce, Susan Resneck, 29
planning, strategic, 77, 94, 100–104
polarities vs. problems, 46
Positive Academic Leadership (Buller), 71
positive framing, 85, 86
power: in academia, 35–40; accepting, 35, 37–40; approaches to, 35; boundaries, 23, 39–40, 43; and budget responsibility, 108; and clarity of communications, 40–43; and conflict management, 43–46, 52; constraints on, 38; formal, 35–36, 38–39; informal/soft, 36, 38–39; inventorying, 37–38; personal, 39; questions on, 52; as structural, 35; of symbolism, 24; and women, 36–37, 48–49. *See also* authority
presentations, 122, 135
presidents: appearance of, 29, 31; author's path, 3–5; communication by, 30–31, 113; contracts for, 138; disruptors as, 79–80; and identity transitions, 18, 19, 29–32; interim, 124; and internal candidates, 126; meeting with, 134–35, 136–37; personal information disclosure, 129–30; role of, 70–71; skills for, 113–14; statistics on, 68; teams for, 31, 114–16
Pressfield, Steven, 90
principal investigators, 106
privacy, 31, 32, 82–83, 129–30, 131
problems: and changes, 74–77; vs. polarities, 46; and vision, 92
profits, 6, 69
program directors, 106
prospectus, 117–18, 120, 124, 126, 128, 130, 131
public figure, transition to, 19, 23–24, 29, 30–31
public speaking, 79, 99

queer women, 28, 122–23, 129, 136. *See also* first, being

race. *See* women of color
radiating energetic state, 61, 65
references, 43, 123, 130

rejection, 20–21, 127, 137–38

relationships: and fund-raising skills, 112; leadership as relational, 73, 86; mentoring/career, 1, 10–11, 145; paradigms, 51–52; power dynamics, 23, 39–40, 43; and presidency, 113; with president, 134–35; and team-building, 114–16; with trustees, 29. *See also* family and spouses; friends; peer groups

resistance, managing, 43–44, 50–52

responsibility: budget, 106–8, 112–13; family, 6, 62; personnel, 106, 110–11, 112–13; of power, 40; revenue, 106, 108–9, 112–13

revenue creation and responsibility skills, 106, 108–9, 112–13

Rhodes College, 5, 73, 76, 102, 119, 134, 136–37

risk: and decision-making, 82; and job searches, 127, 136, 142; as leadership trait/skill, 6, 113; and transitions in identity, 21; and vision, 104

role models, 5, 12, 56, 67–68, 136

ruminating energetic state, 61, 65

salary, 16, 19, 24–25, 123, 138–41

scandals, 113, 114

search committees: and being first, 129, 136; and cover letter and CV, 128; information on, 120, 121–23; and nominations, 125, 127; questions on, 121–22; serving on, 121–22; and vision, 96. *See also* interviews

search consultants and firms: application steps, 127–29; author's experiences, 8, 119; feedback from, 138; influence of, 124; as information resource, 119, 124, 138, 142; liaison role, 117, 118–19; preliminary interviews with, 129; questions for, 121–24; reasons for using, 117–20; resources on, 119. *See also* interviews

searches, job: acceptance expectations, 124, 133, 136–37; application steps, 127–29; author's experiences, 8, 119, 134; deal-breaker requests, 123–24, 134; deciding to apply, 120–24; and fit, 135–36; as internal candidate, 124–27, 140; luck and risk in, 127, 136, 141–42;

personal information disclosure in, 129–30; presentations for, 122, 135; questions for, 121–24, 125–27, 142–43; reference checks, 123, 130; rejections, 20–21, 127, 137–38; resources on, 119; responding to offers, 138–41; and salary, 123, 138–41; timeline for, 123; withdrawing from, 126, 137. *See also* interviews; prospectus; search committees; search consultants and firms

secrecy, 55, 65, 82–83

self-examination: assessing leadership readiness, 7; assessing skills, 112–13; importance of, 144–46; and transitions, 17–19, 32–33

sexism: examples of, 6; in interviews, 135–36; responses to, 36–37. *See also* first, being

shame, 59, 83

shoes, 81, 133, 135

Siegel, Betty L., 39

sincerity, as virtue, 85, 86

skills: assessing, 112–13; budget, 106–8, 112–13; building, 3, 105–6; fund-raising, 106, 111–13; and gender, 68–69; media skills, 30, 31; personnel, 106, 110–11, 112–13, 114–16; for presidency, 113–14; questions on, 112–13, 116; revenue, 106, 108–9, 112–13; storytelling, 100; and vision, 93

Skoal, Vibe, 147n2

social media, 57

speeches, 79

sponsors, career, 10–11, 145

spouses. *See* family and spouses

Steffy, Jim, 7–8

Storbeck, Shelly, 8, 119

storytelling, 53–54, 100, 104, 131

strategic planning, 77, 94, 100–104

strategic thinking, 102–3

stress: breadwinner, 25; and energy management, 60; and happiness, 12, 57–59, 65; of job searches, 142; of leadership, 15, 28, 109

strictness, as virtue, 85, 86

student affairs, 16, 106, 108

students, 70, 77, 83, 121–22

successes, 16, 27, 53–54, 66, 72, 78, 145

sui generis transition, 19, 30

Sun Tzu, 85–86, 88
supporters, career, 10
symbols, 19, 23–24, 29, 104

teams, 18, 19–20, 31, 114–16
tears and crying, 49–50
tenure, 34–35, 141
terminations. *See* firing
Thomas-Stillmann model, 44–45
time: and job searches, 123, 131; managing, 20, 24, 31–32, 96–97; pressures of leadership, 15, 16; and strategic planning, 103; and vision, 95–96
transformation, in vision, 93
transitions. *See* identity, transitions in
transparency, 55, 82–83
travel, 63–64
Troutt, Bill, 73
trustees. *See* board of trustees
truth, 55, 57
Truth without Tears (Hodges and Welsh), 99

urgency and creating change, 77, 78–79

vacations, 63–64
vice presidents: as first jump role, 16; and internal candidates, 124, 127; and searches, 117, 118, 121, 122, 124, 134; skills for, 108, 113–14; and team-building, 114–16
virtues, 83–87, 88
vision: communicating, 98–100; creating, 93–94; and creativity, 12, 96–98, 104;

and decision-making, 82, 90; defined, 91–92; engaging others, 94, 95, 98–100, 104; vs. goals, 92–93, 101; mistakes in, 89–90, 94–95; and pillars of mission, business model, and culture, 90–91, 96, 97, 98, 104; premature, 95, 96, 97; questions on, 93, 94, 97–98, 103, 104; storytelling on, 100, 104; and strategic planning, 94, 100–103; as term, 102; timing of, 95–96; vision statements, 91

The Way of Transition (Bridges), 17
Welsh, Olga M., 99
wife paradigm, 51–52
Wigginton, Russ, 73
wine and cheese budget, 38–39, 108
wisdom, as virtue, 85
Wolverton, Mimi, 39
women: family expectations of, 6, 62; identity concerns, 5, 11–12; lack of models for, 12, 67–68; and personal criticism, 57; positive effects of female leadership, 2, 6–7; resistance to power of, 36–37; statistics on, 5–6. *See also* first, being; queer women; women of color
Women at the Top (Wolverton et al.), 39
women of color: and anger, 47, 48–49; and appearance, 26; peer groups, 28–29; and salary equity, 140; and searches, 122–23, 129, 135–36. *See also* first, being
work-life alignment, 62–64

yes, saying, 41

DISCOVER MORE BOOKS
IN THE HIGHER ED LEADERSHIP ESSENTIALS SERIES

 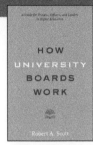   

 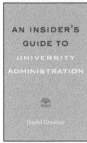 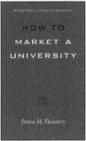

HOW TO RUN A COLLEGE

A Practical Guide for Trustees, Faculty, Administrators, and Policymakers

Brian C. Mitchell and W. Joseph King

HOW UNIVERSITY BOARDS WORK

A Guide for Trustees, Officers, and Leaders in Higher Education

Robert A. Scott

INVESTIGATING COLLEGE STUDENT MISCONDUCT

Oren R. Griffin

HOW TO BE A DEAN

George Justice

HOW BOARDS LEAD SMALL COLLEGES

Alice Lee Williams Brown
with Elizabeth Richmond Hayford

HOW UNIVERSITY BUDGETS WORK

Dean O. Smith

AN INSIDER'S GUIDE TO UNIVERSITY ADMINISTRATION

Daniel Grassian

HOW TO MARKET A UNIVERSITY

Building Value in a Competitive Environment

Teresa M. Flannery

 @JHUPress

 @JohnsHopkins
UniversityPress

 @JHUPress

For more higher education books, visit **press.jhu.edu**